MANDALAS

for Meditation

AN ADULT COLORING BOOK

Vol. 11

Zhena Khasha Books

Copyright © 2015

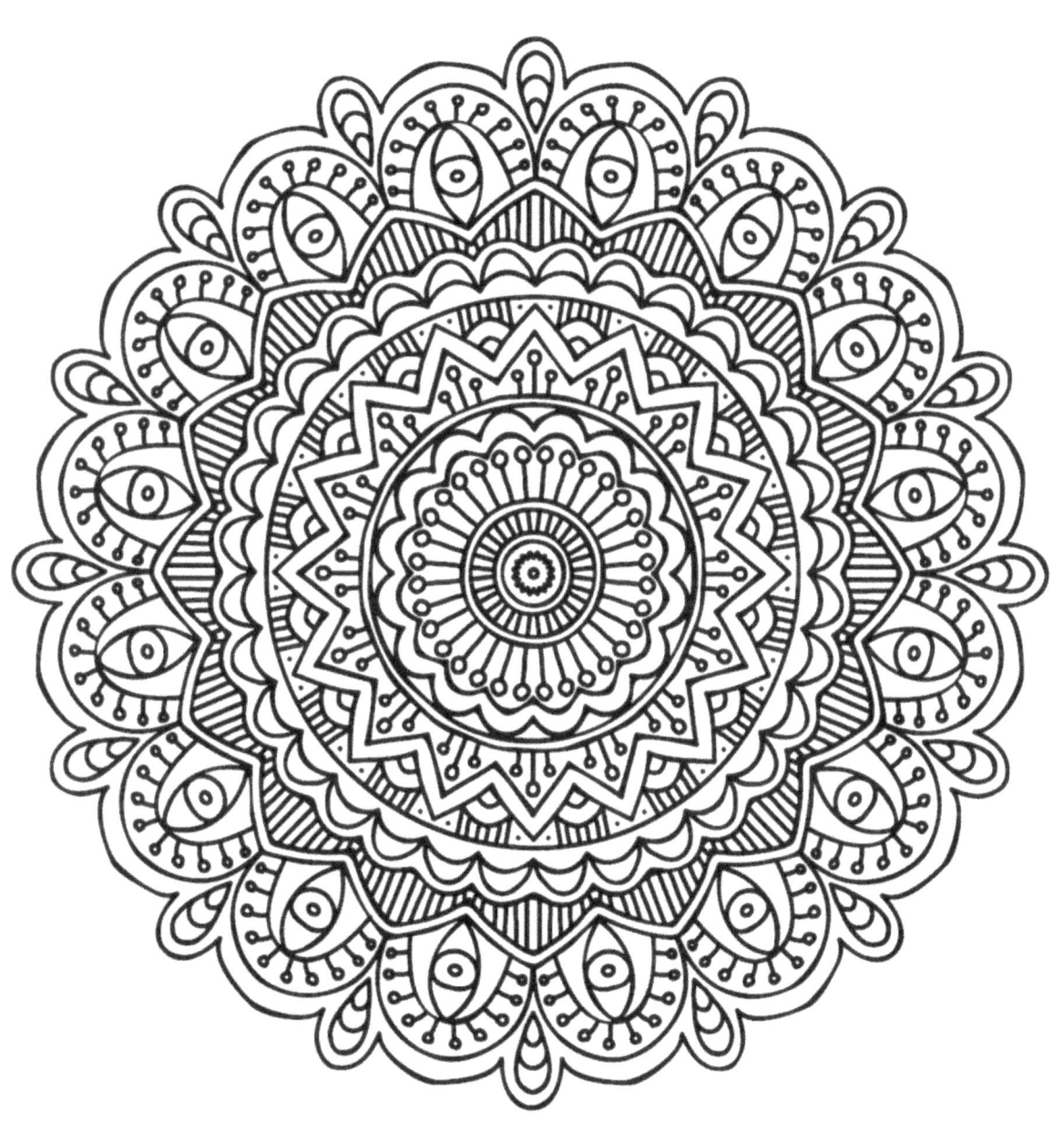

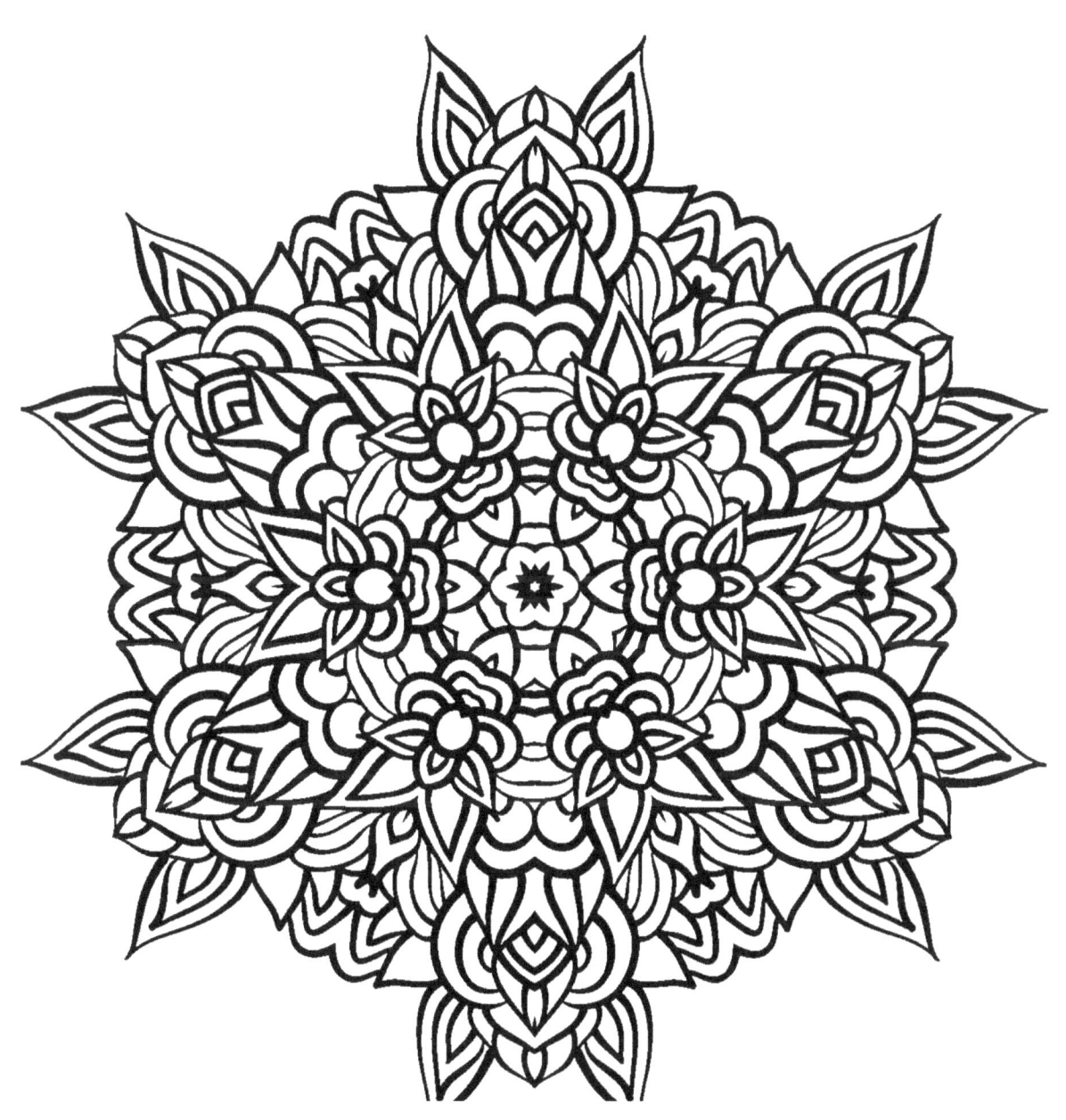

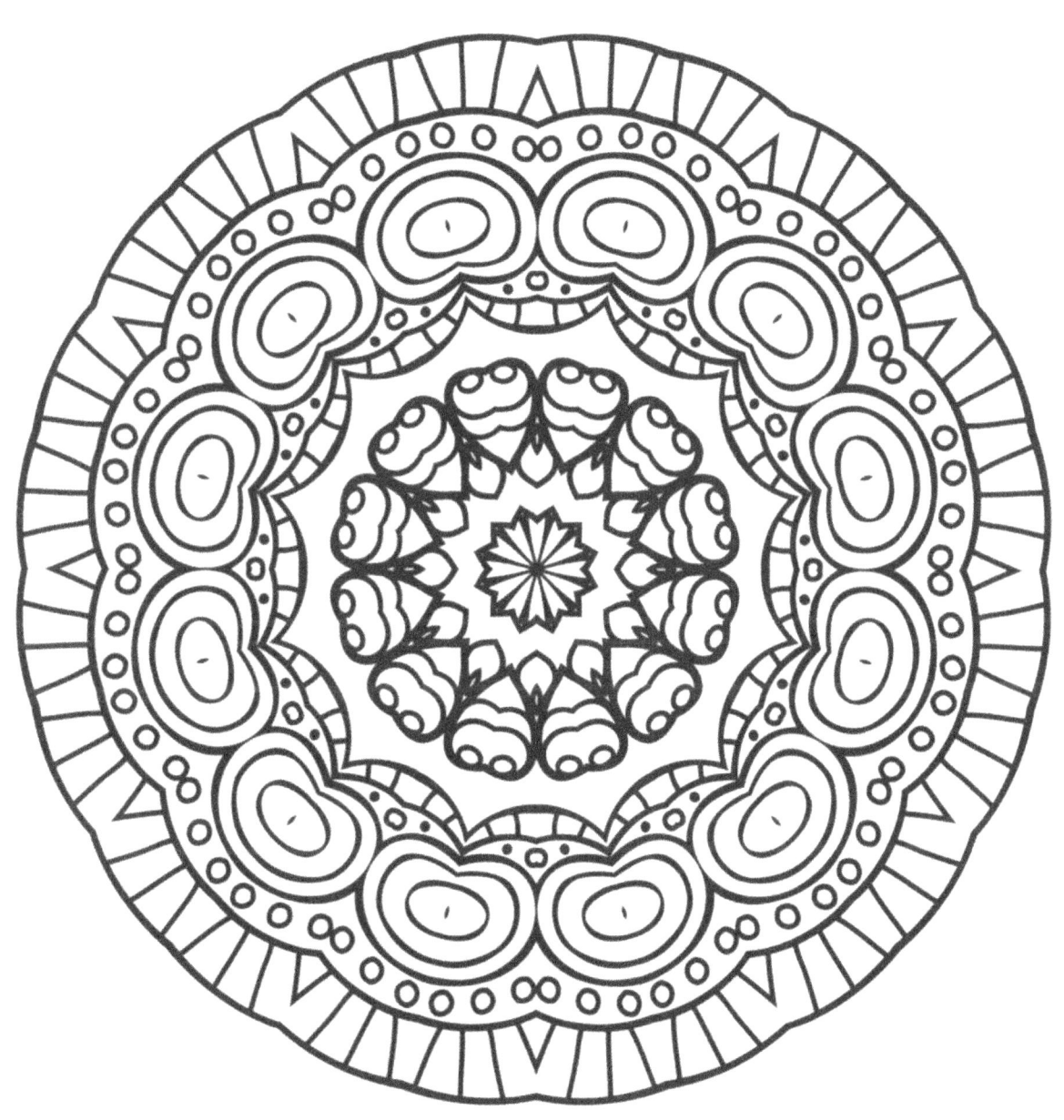

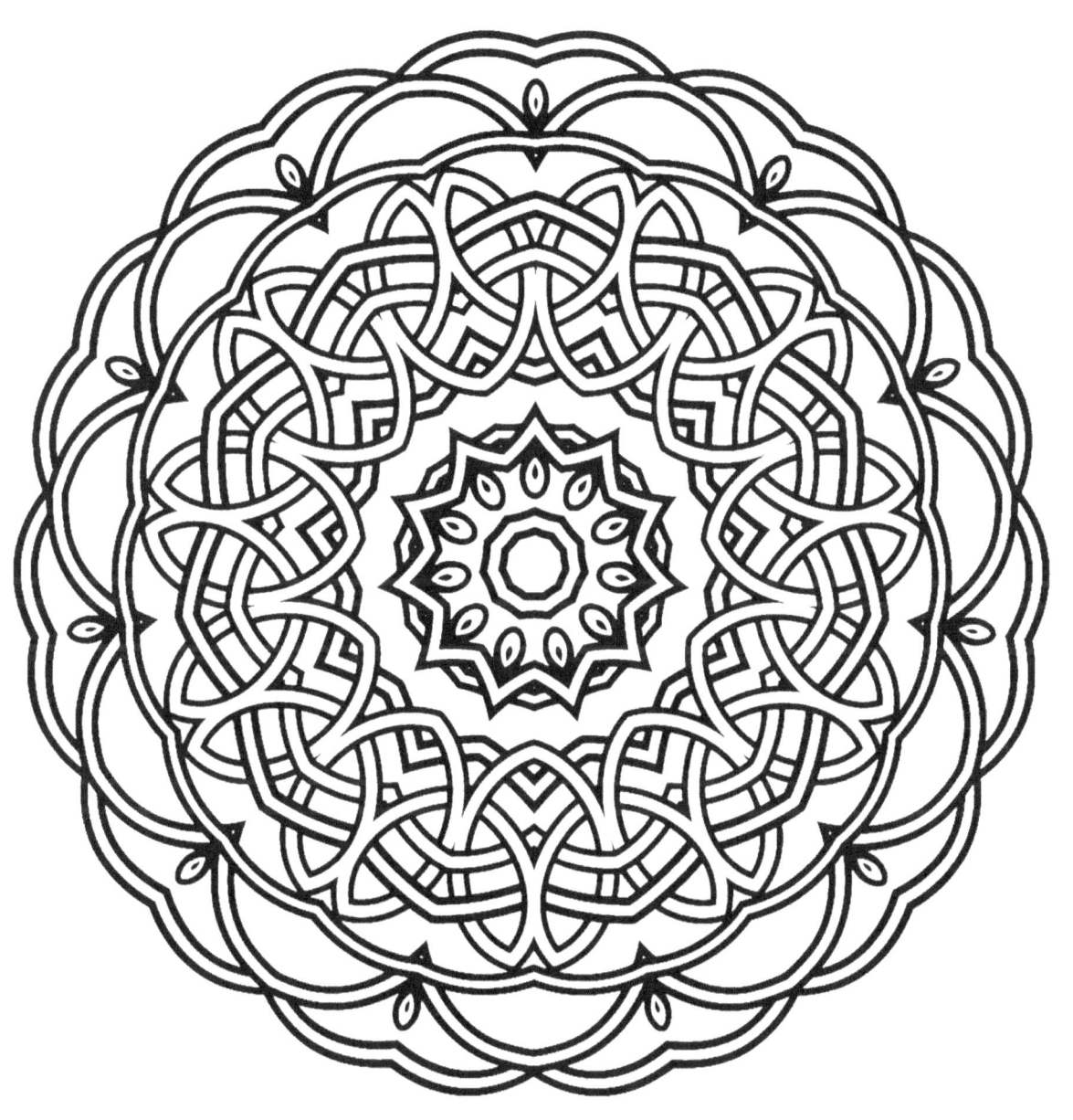

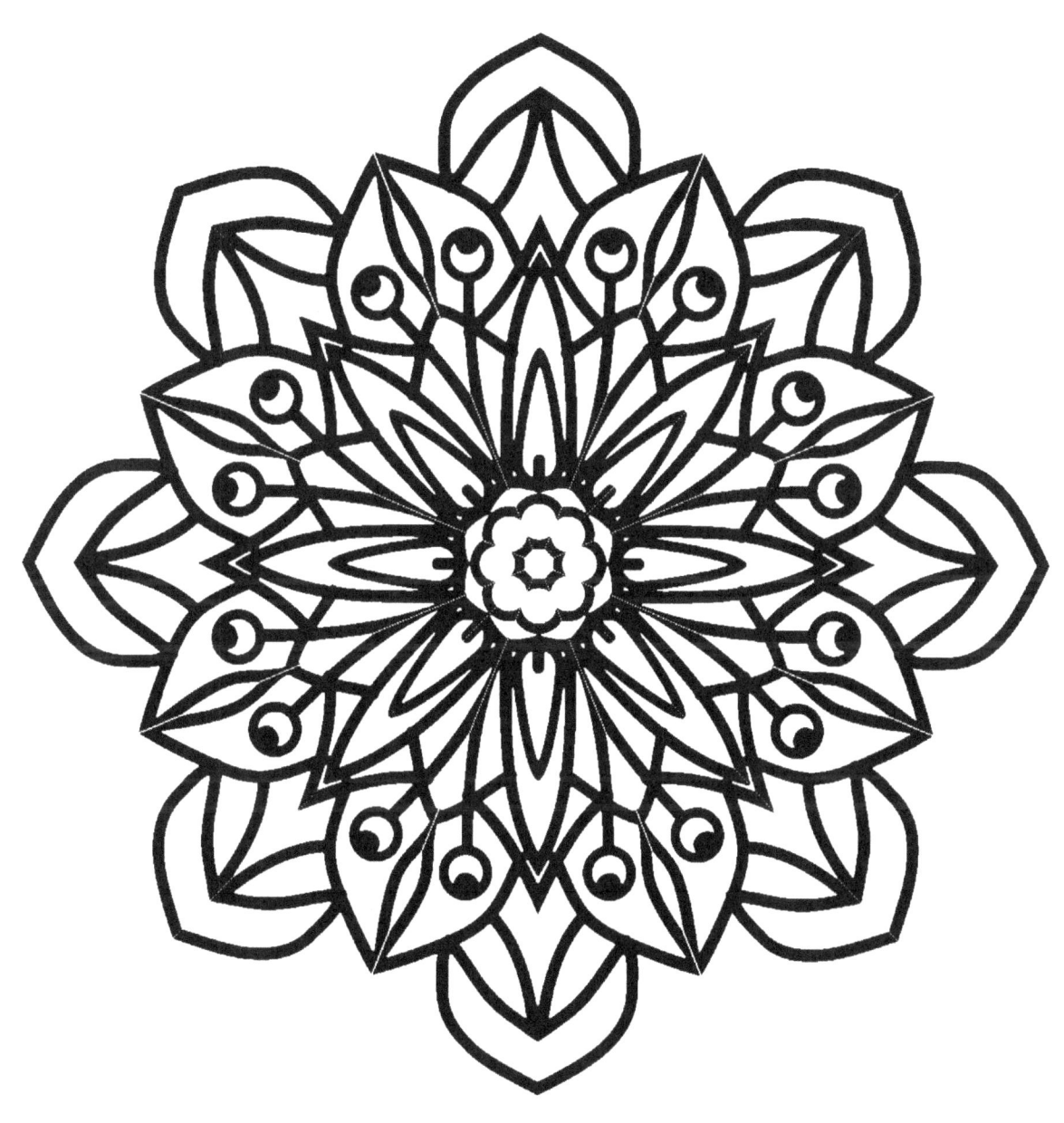

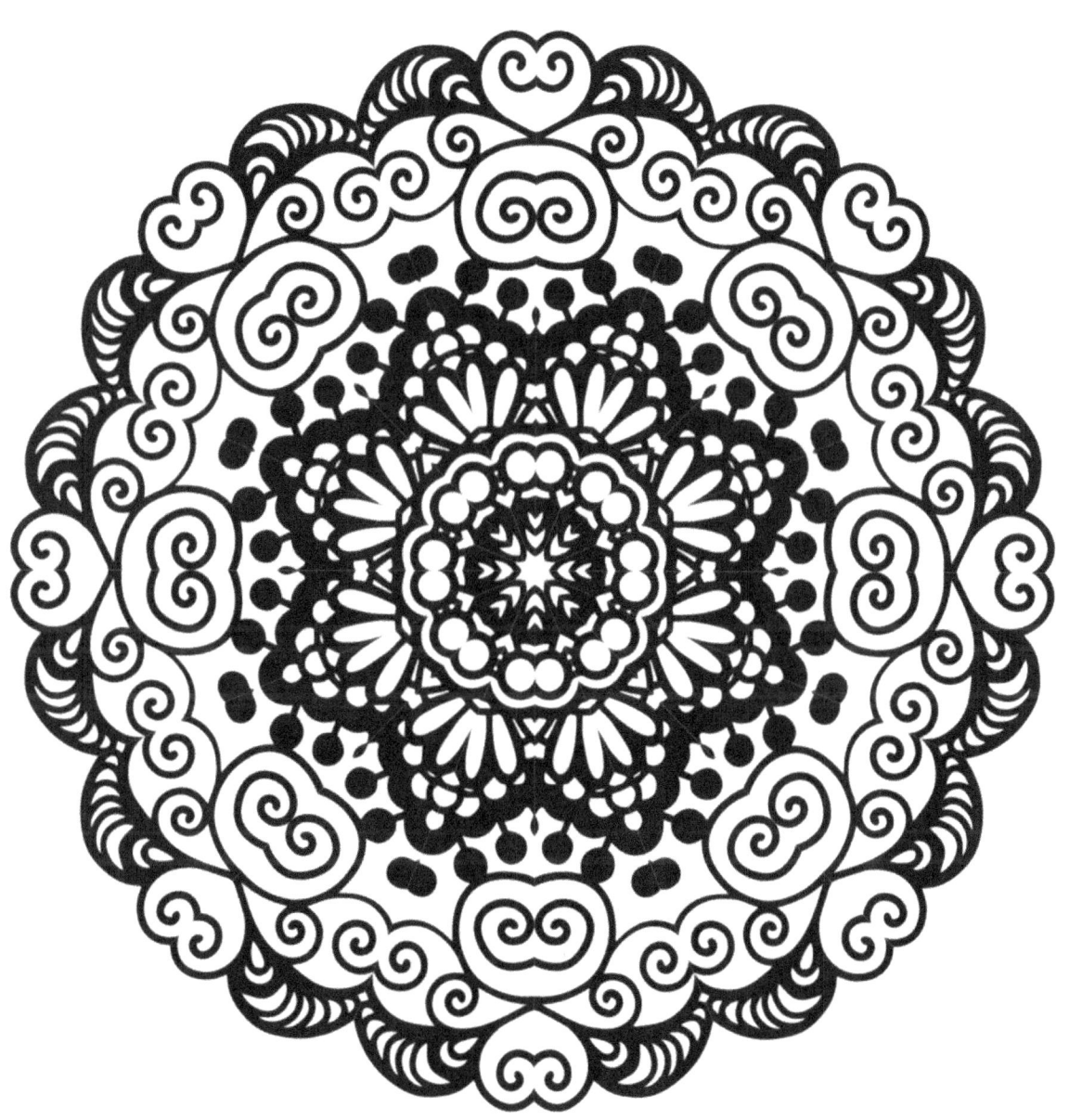

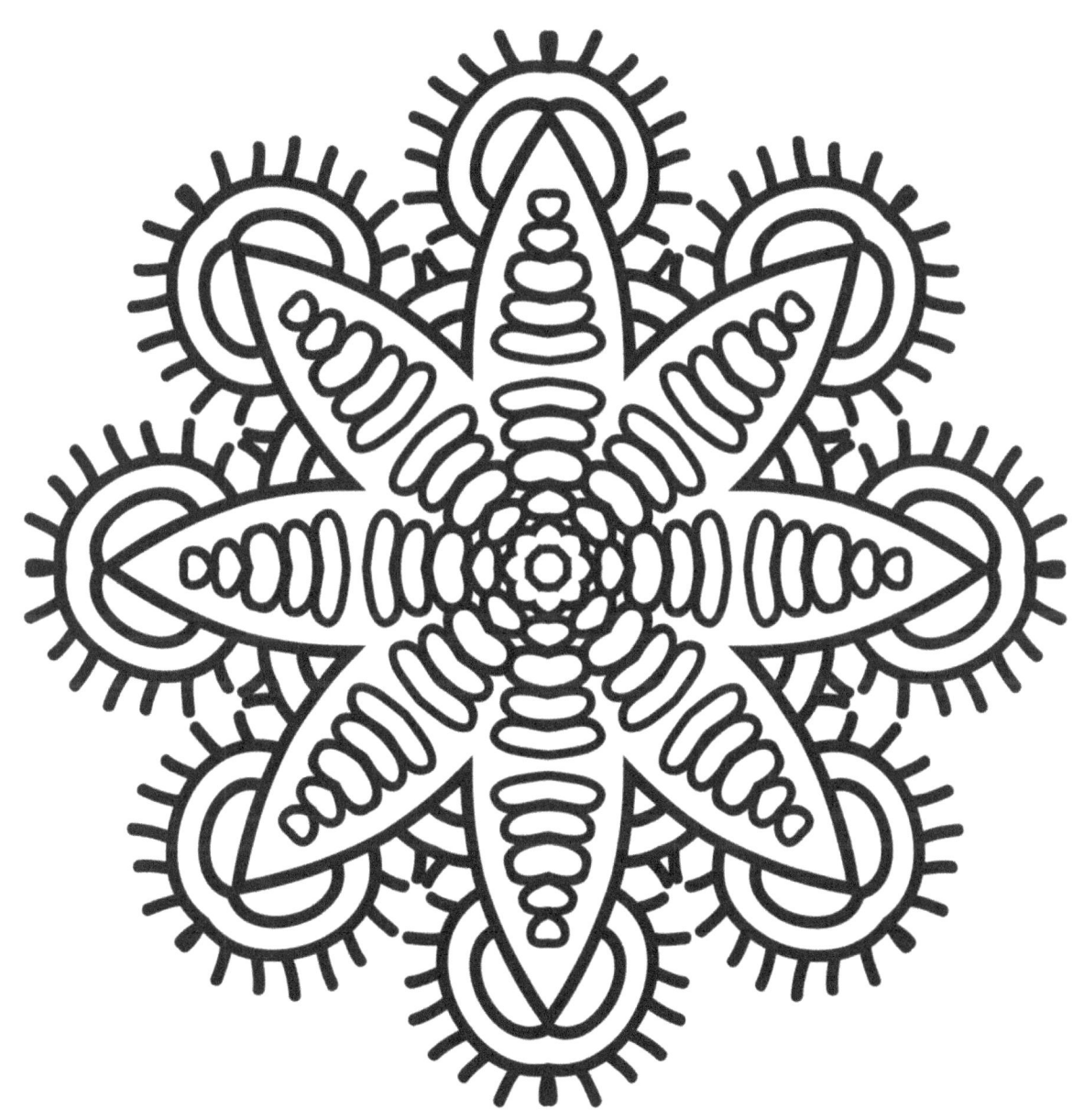

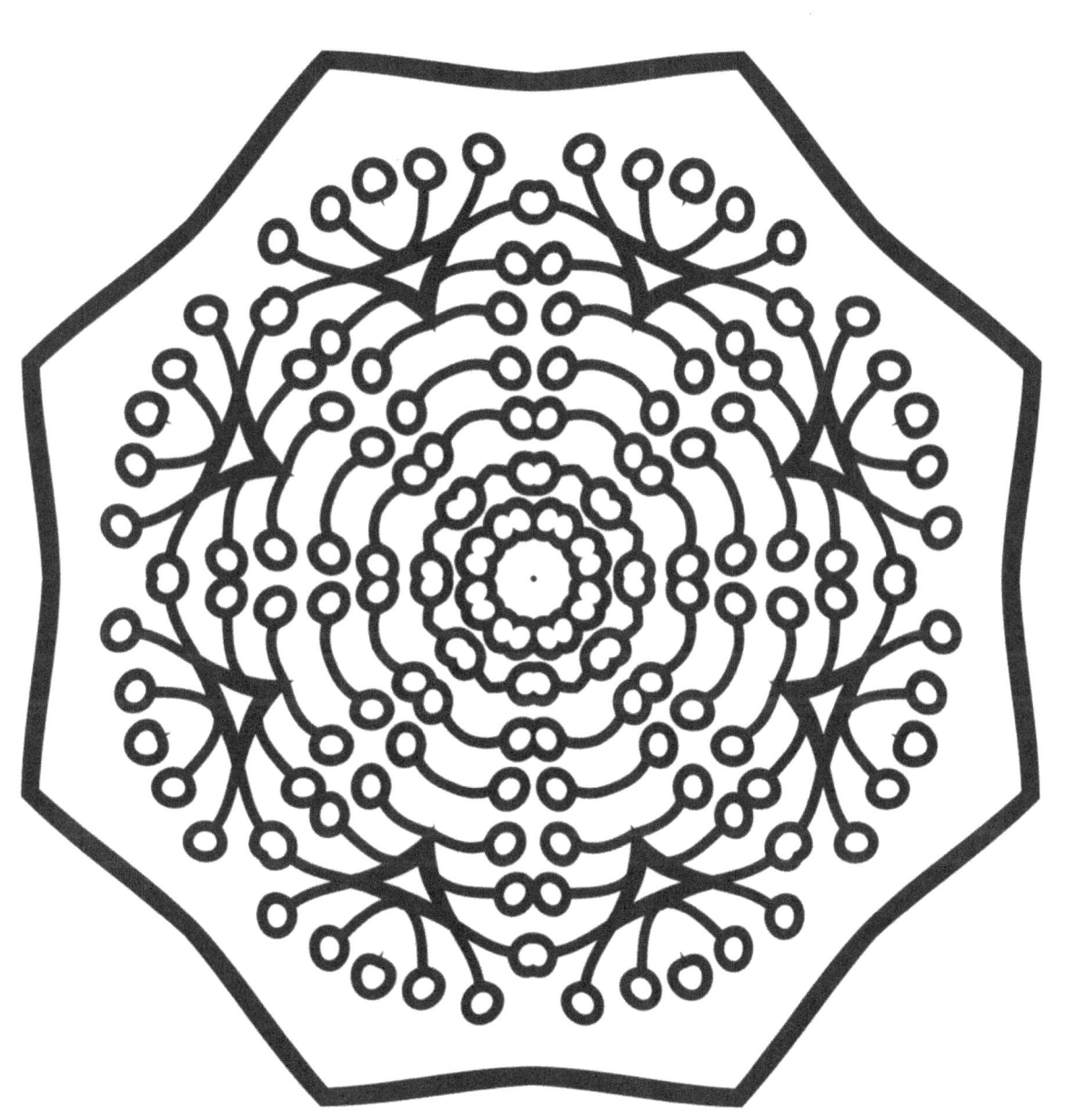

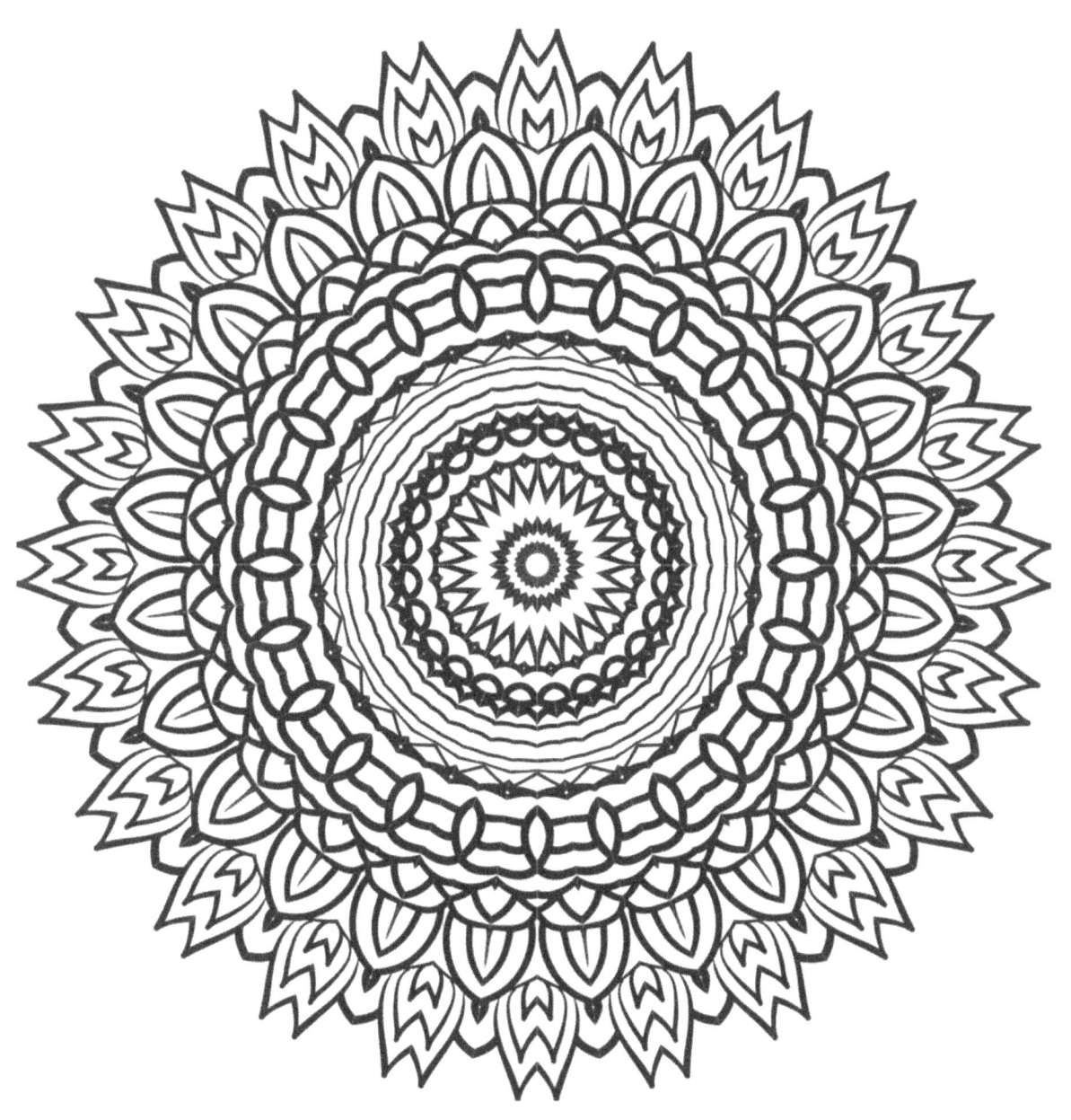

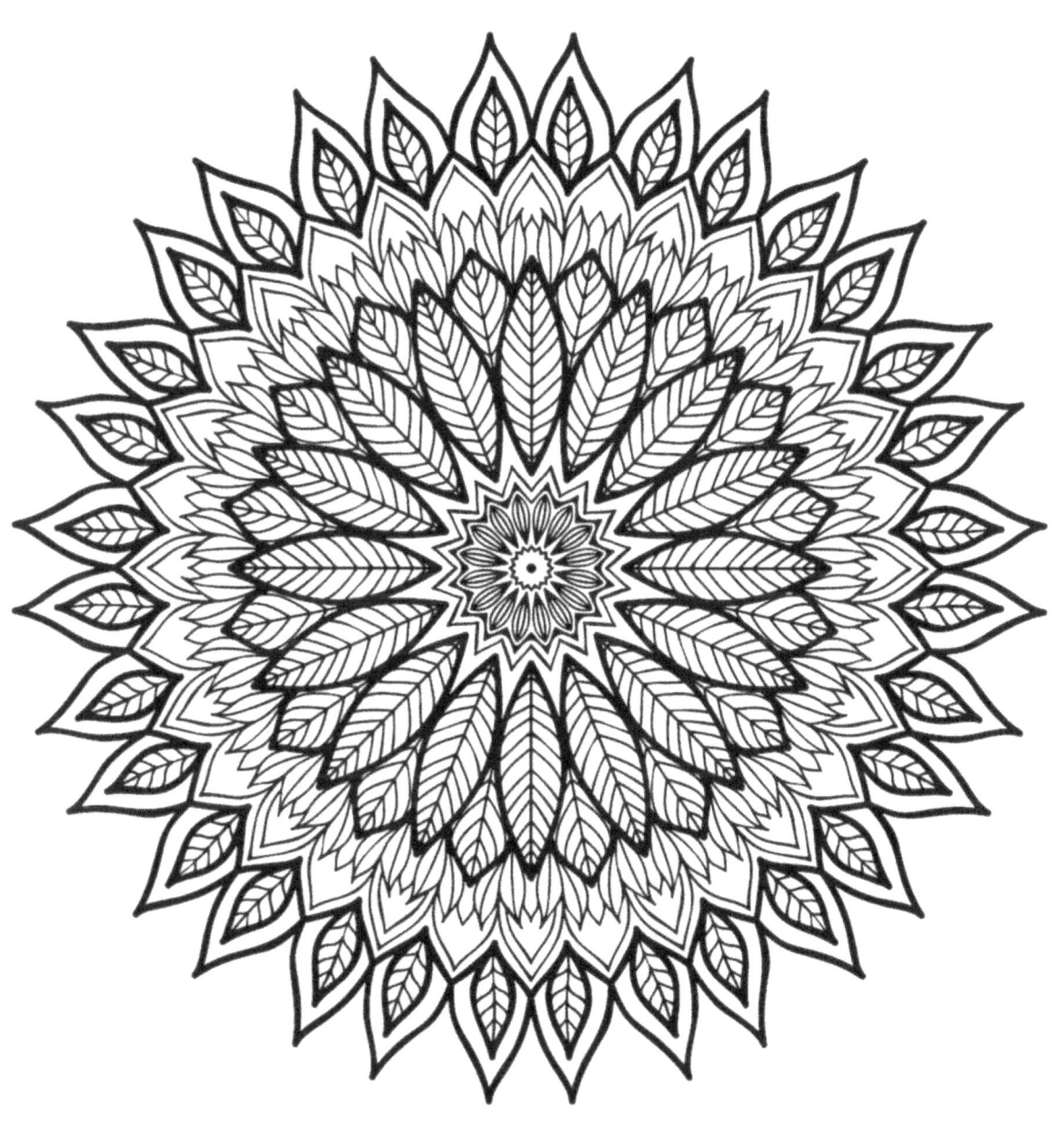

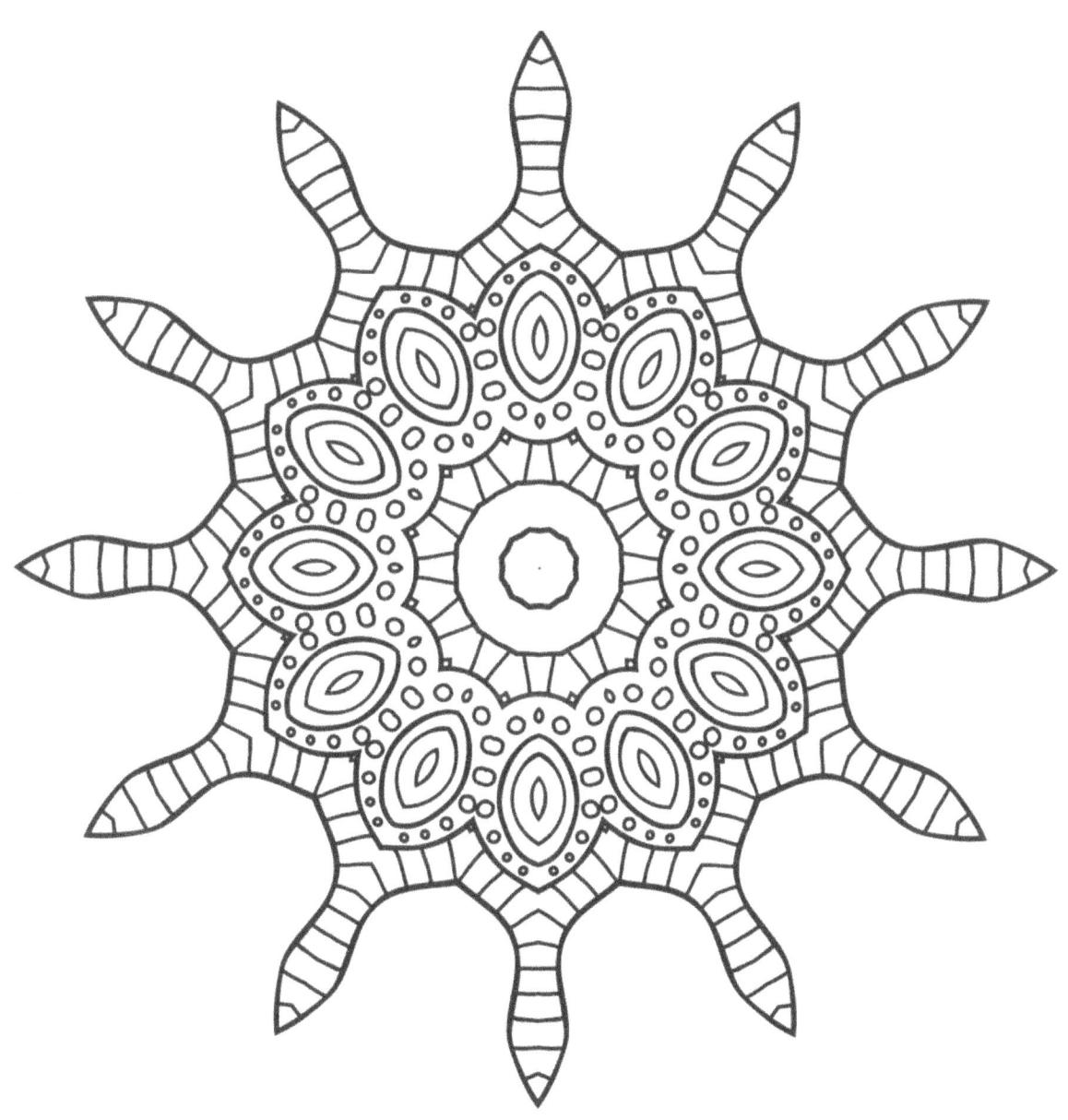

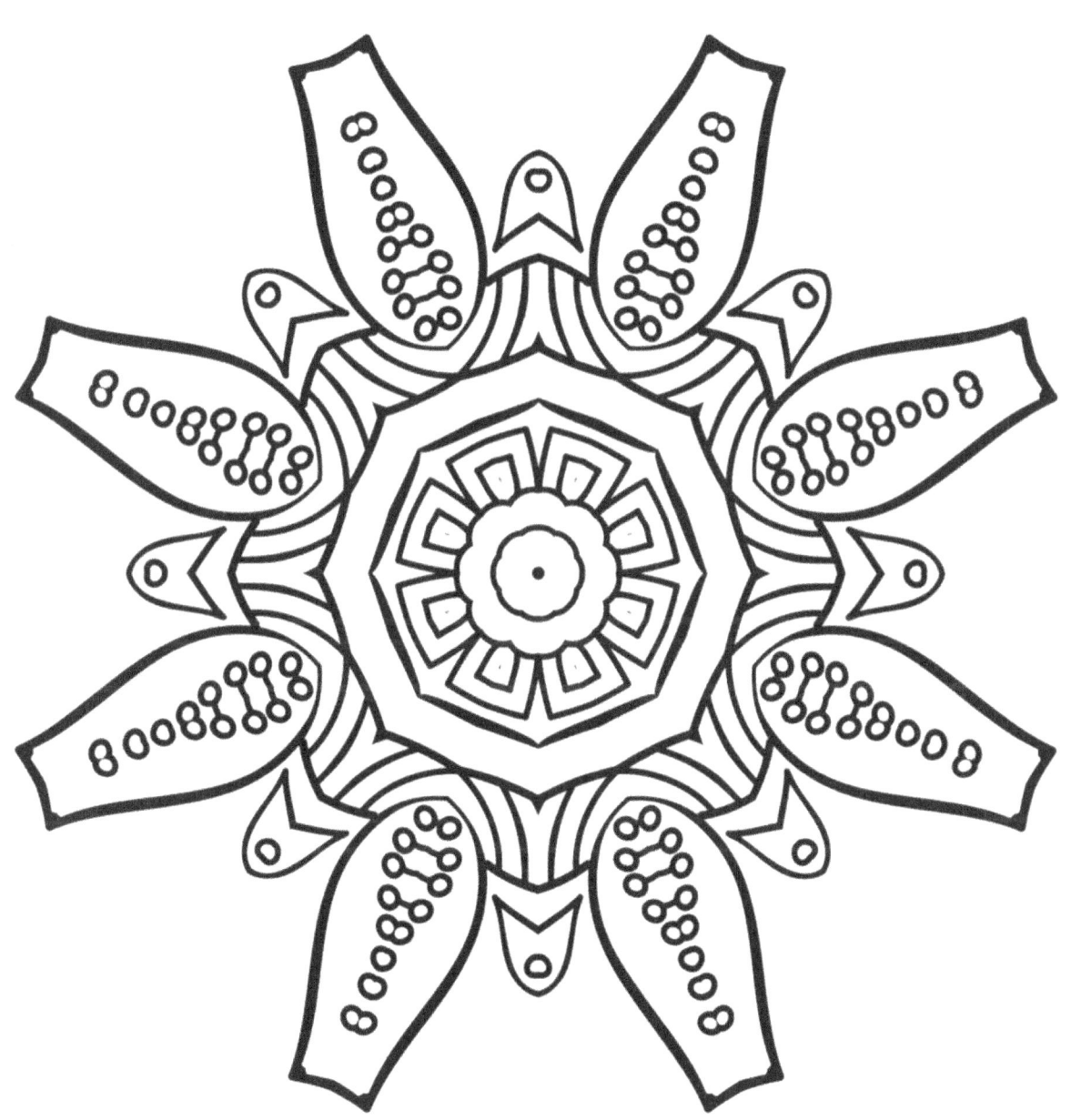

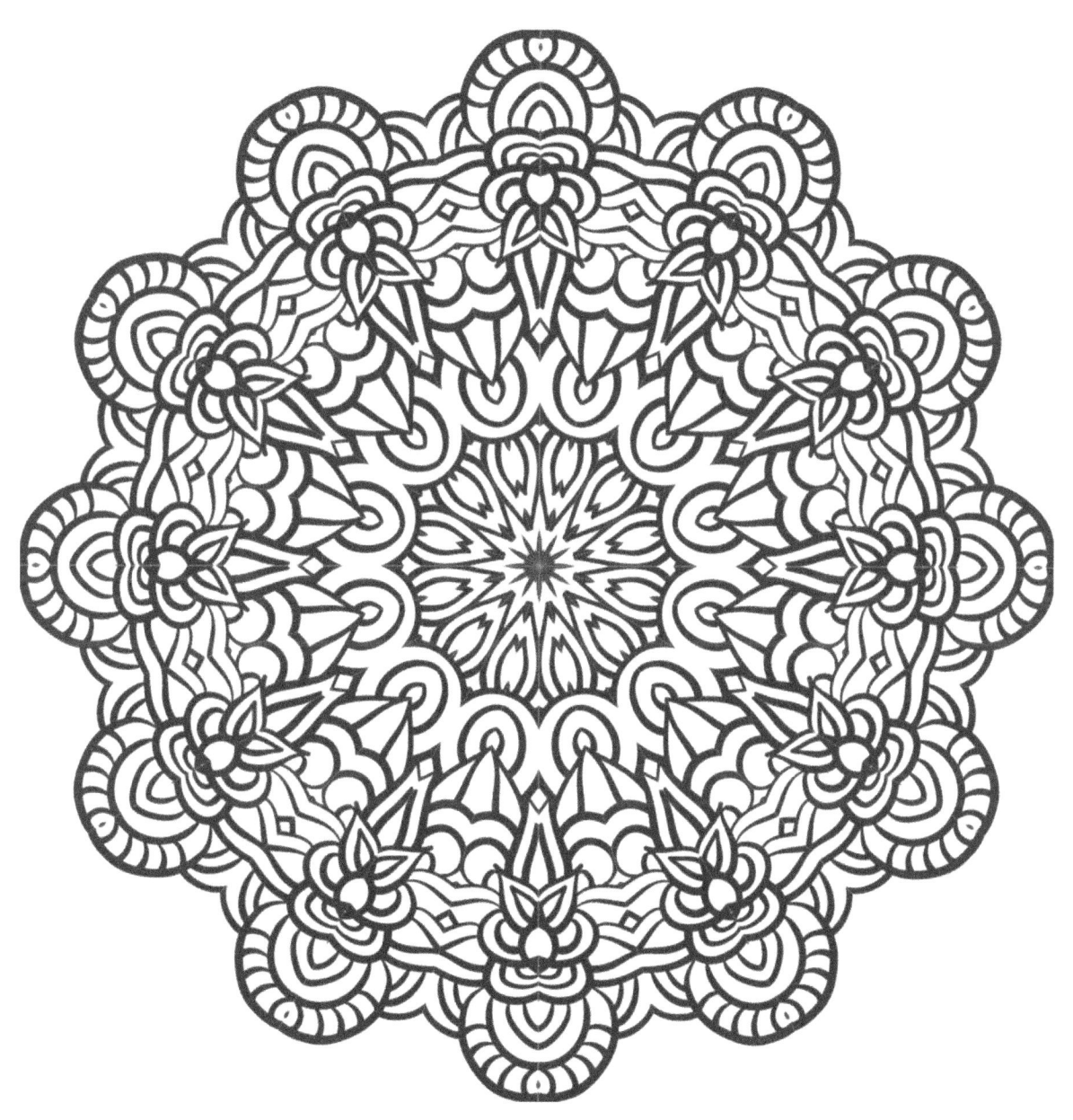

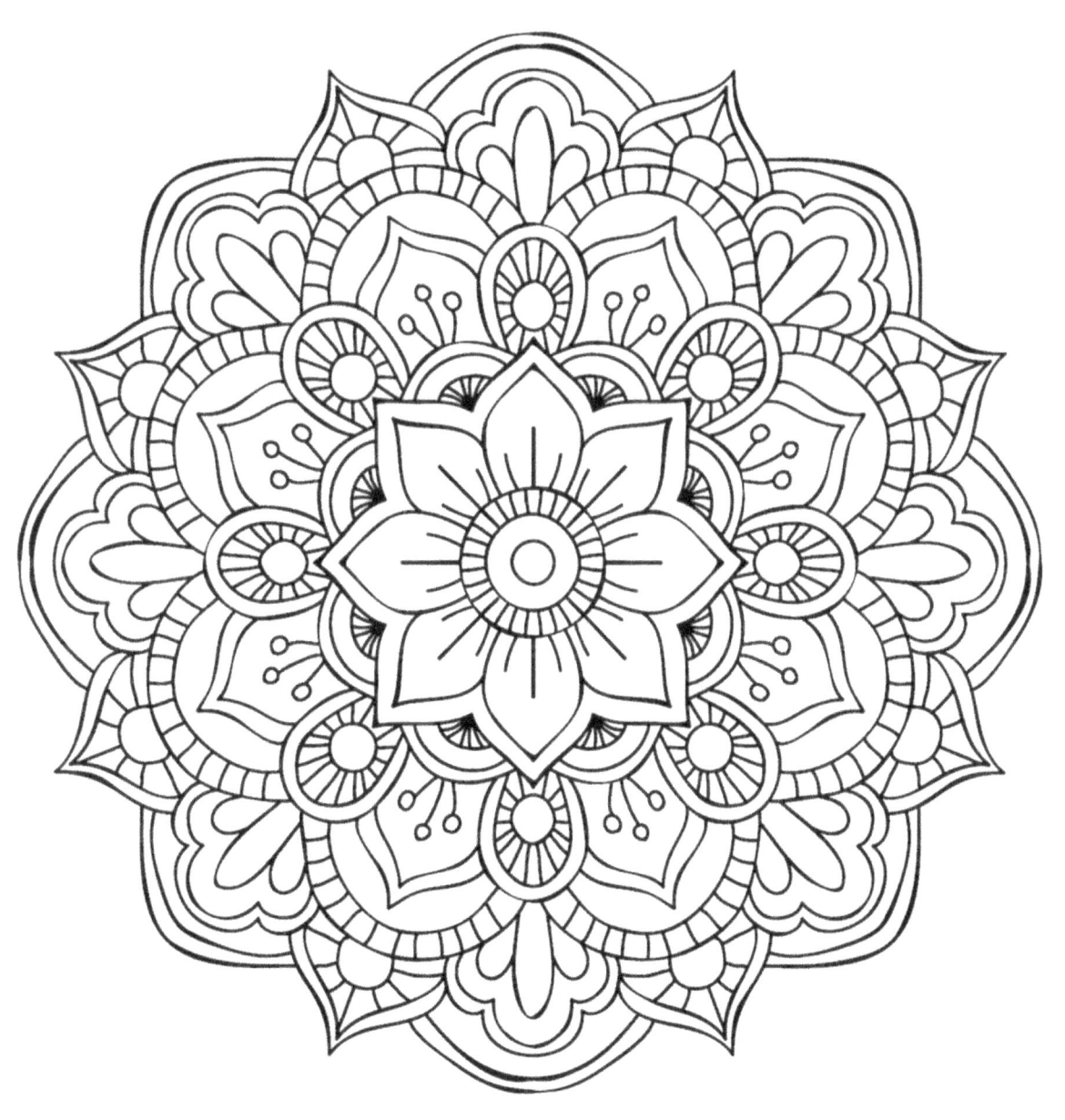

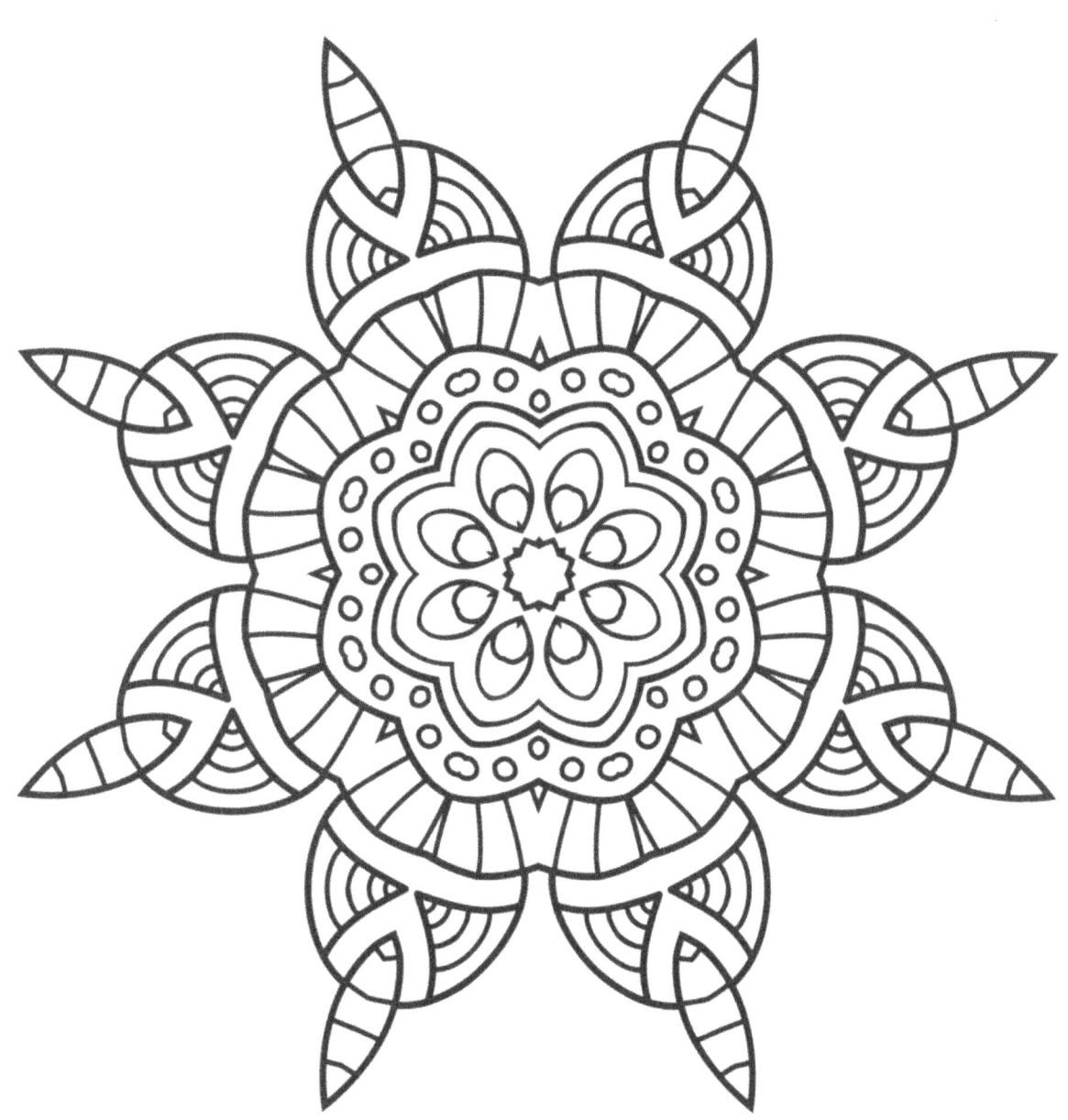

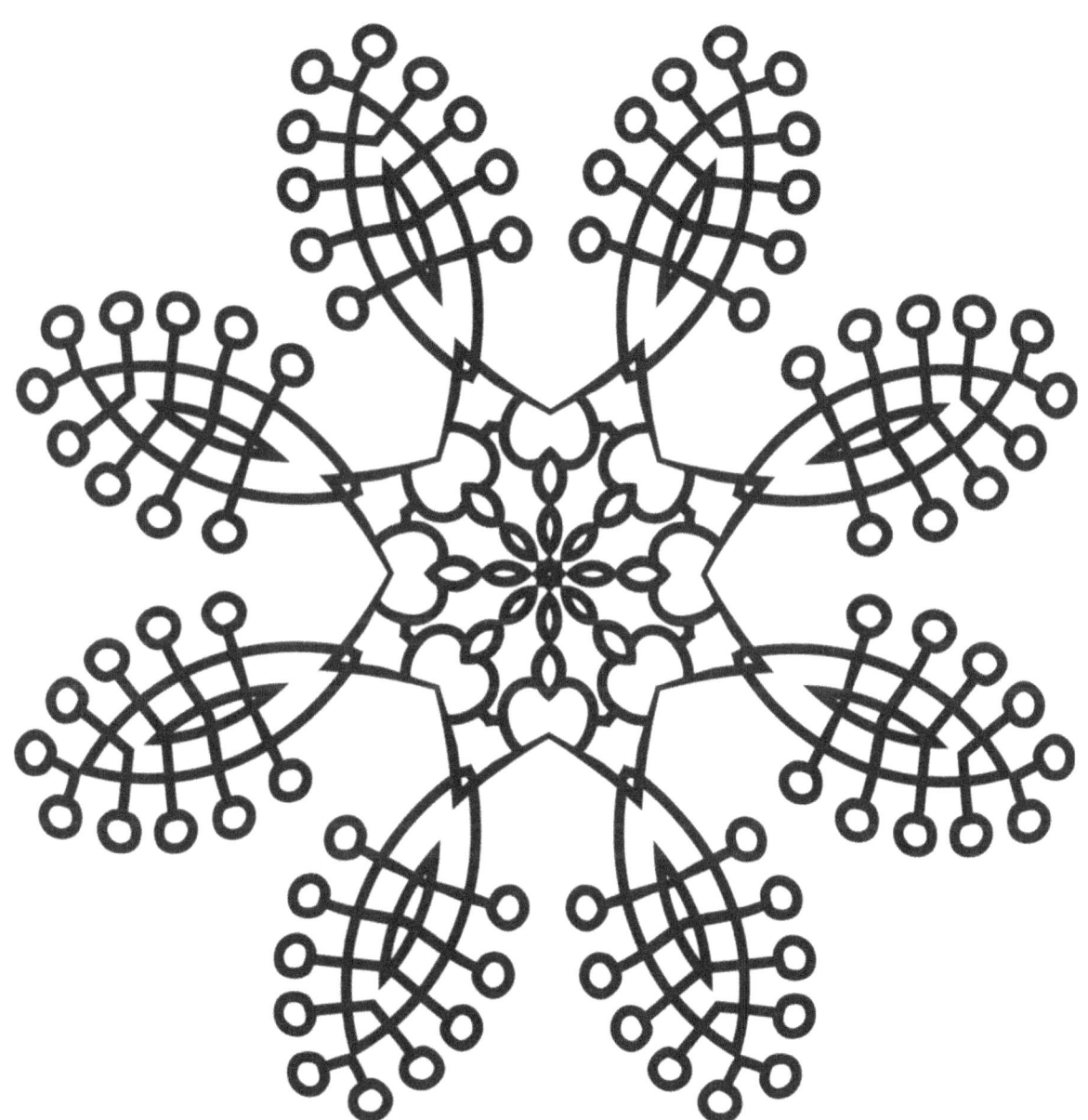

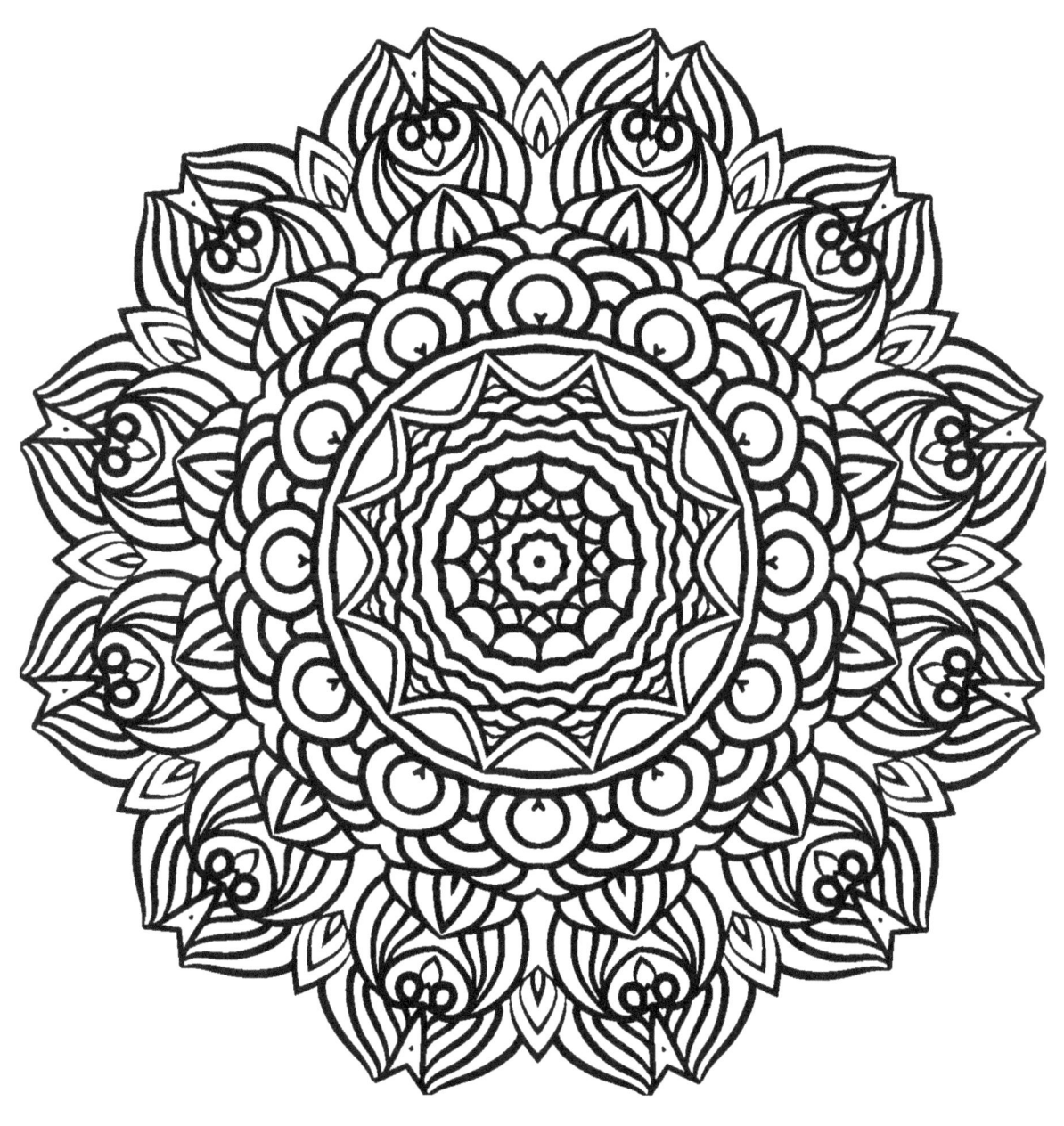

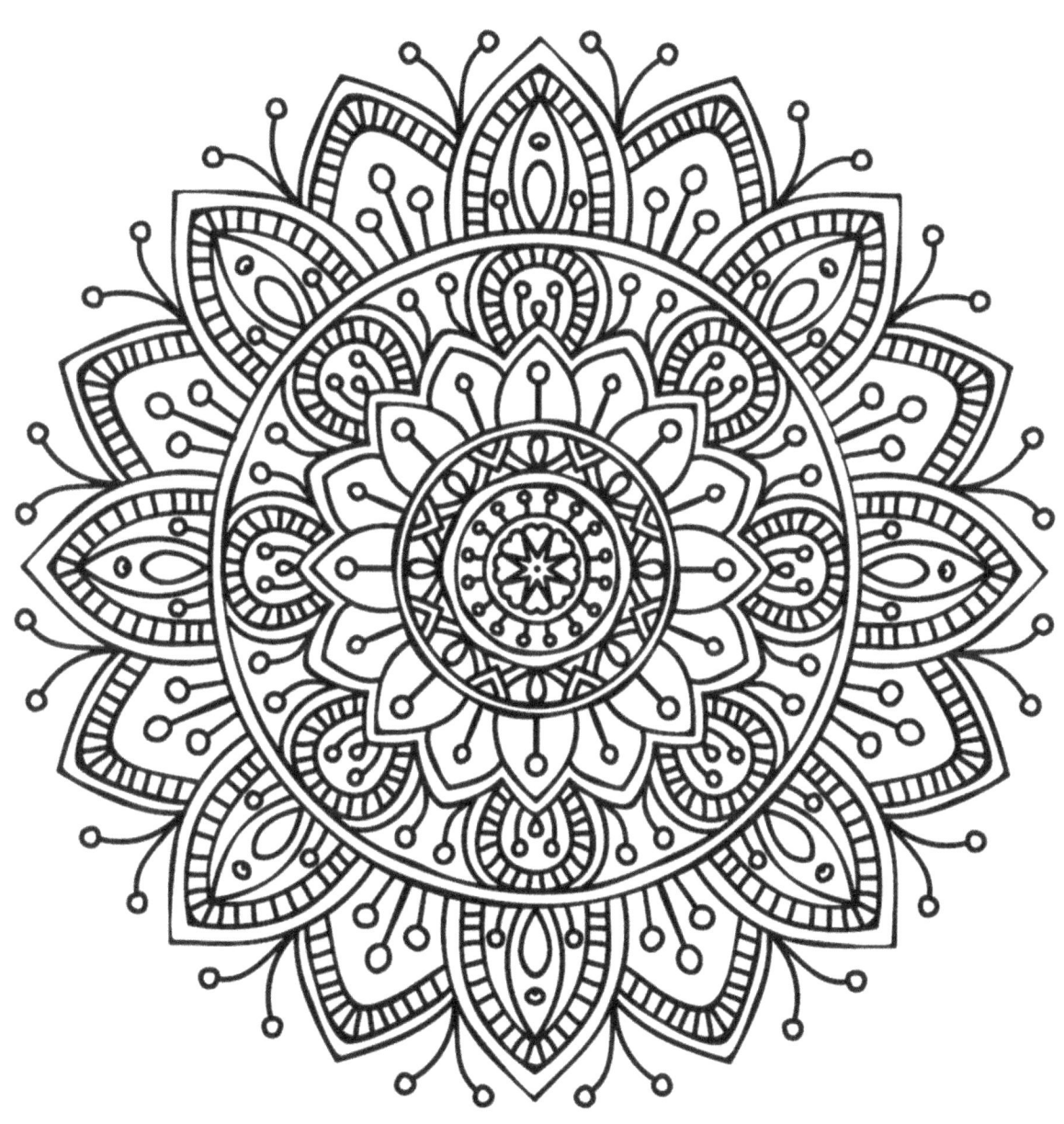

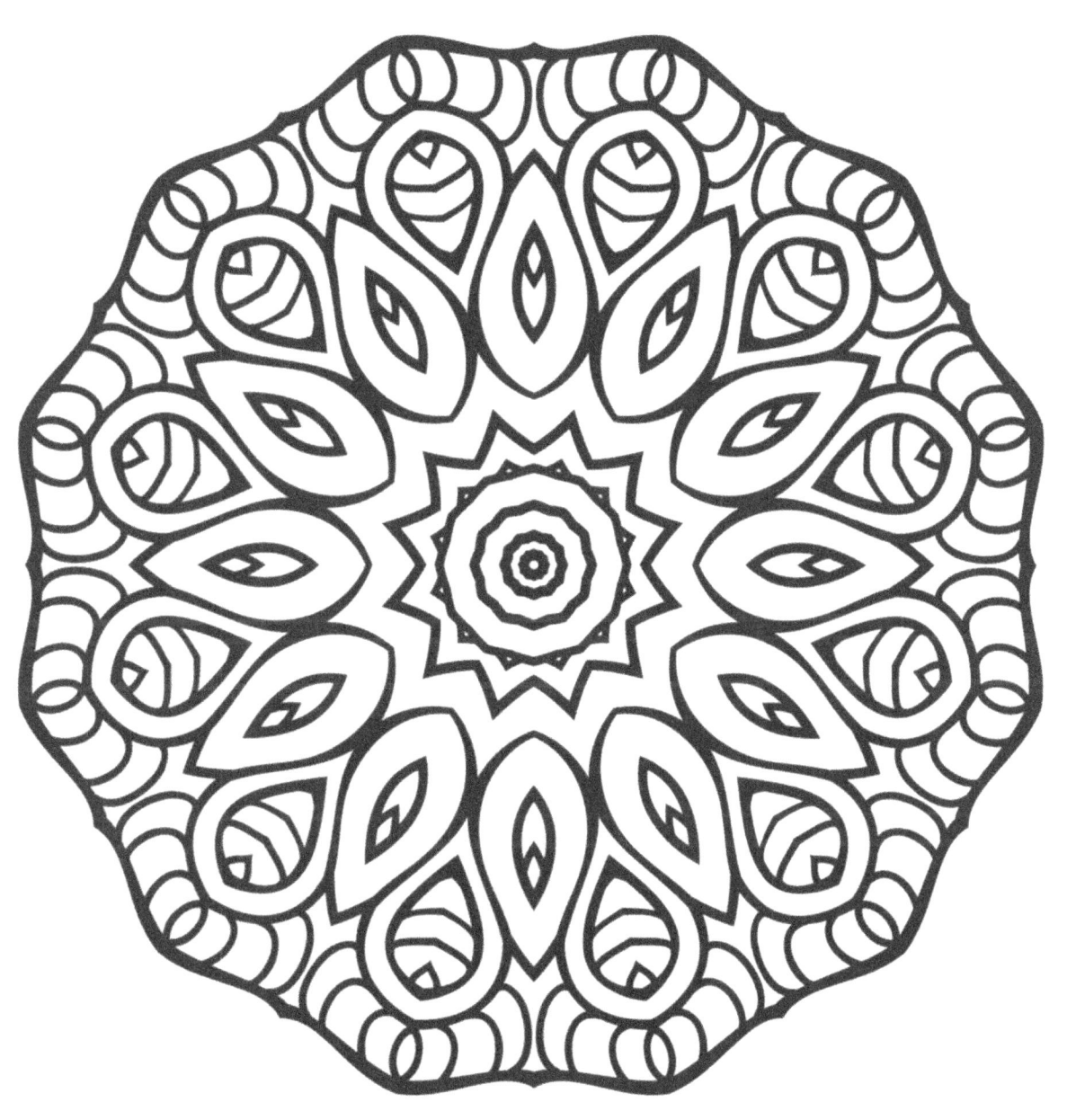

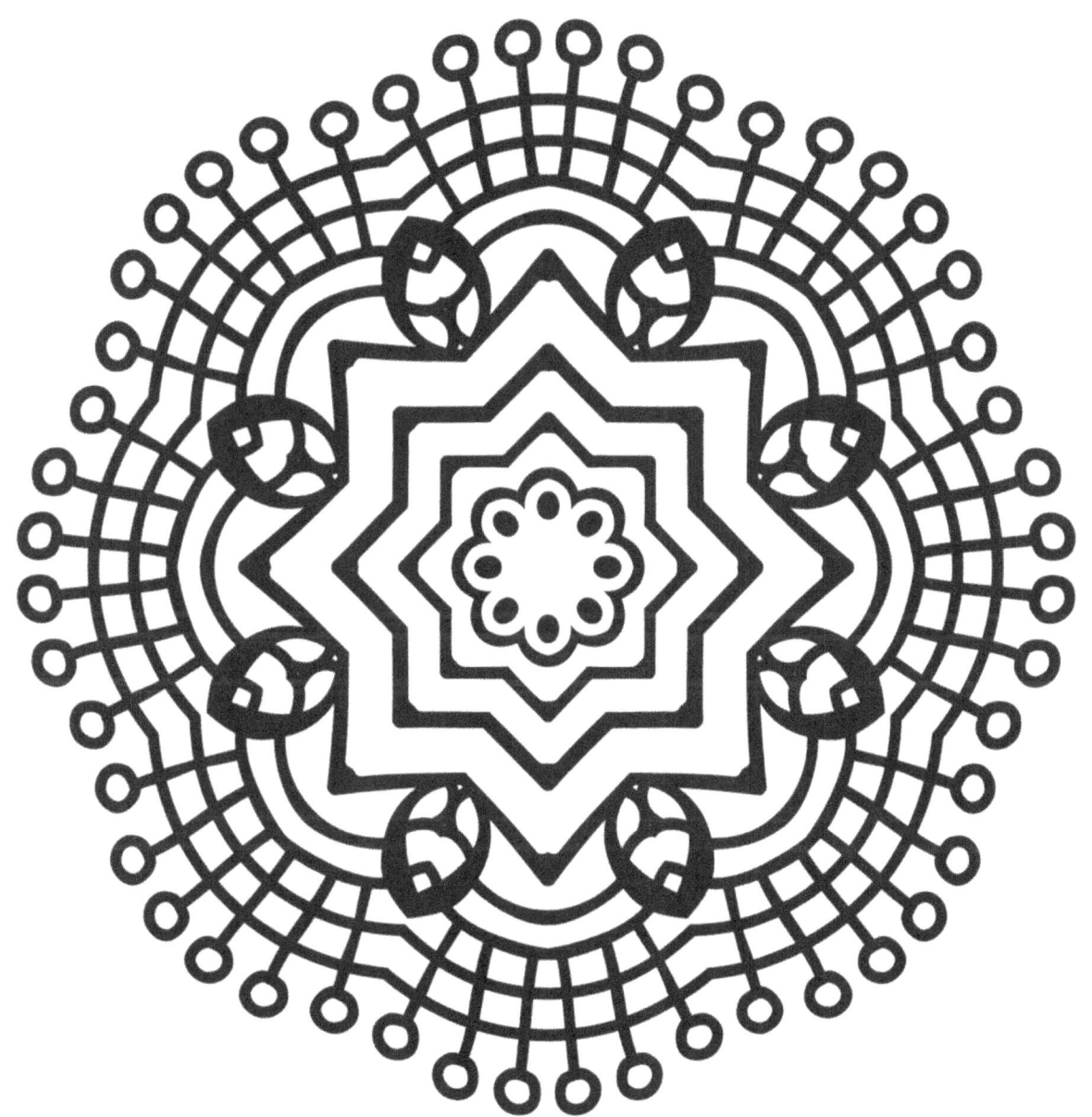

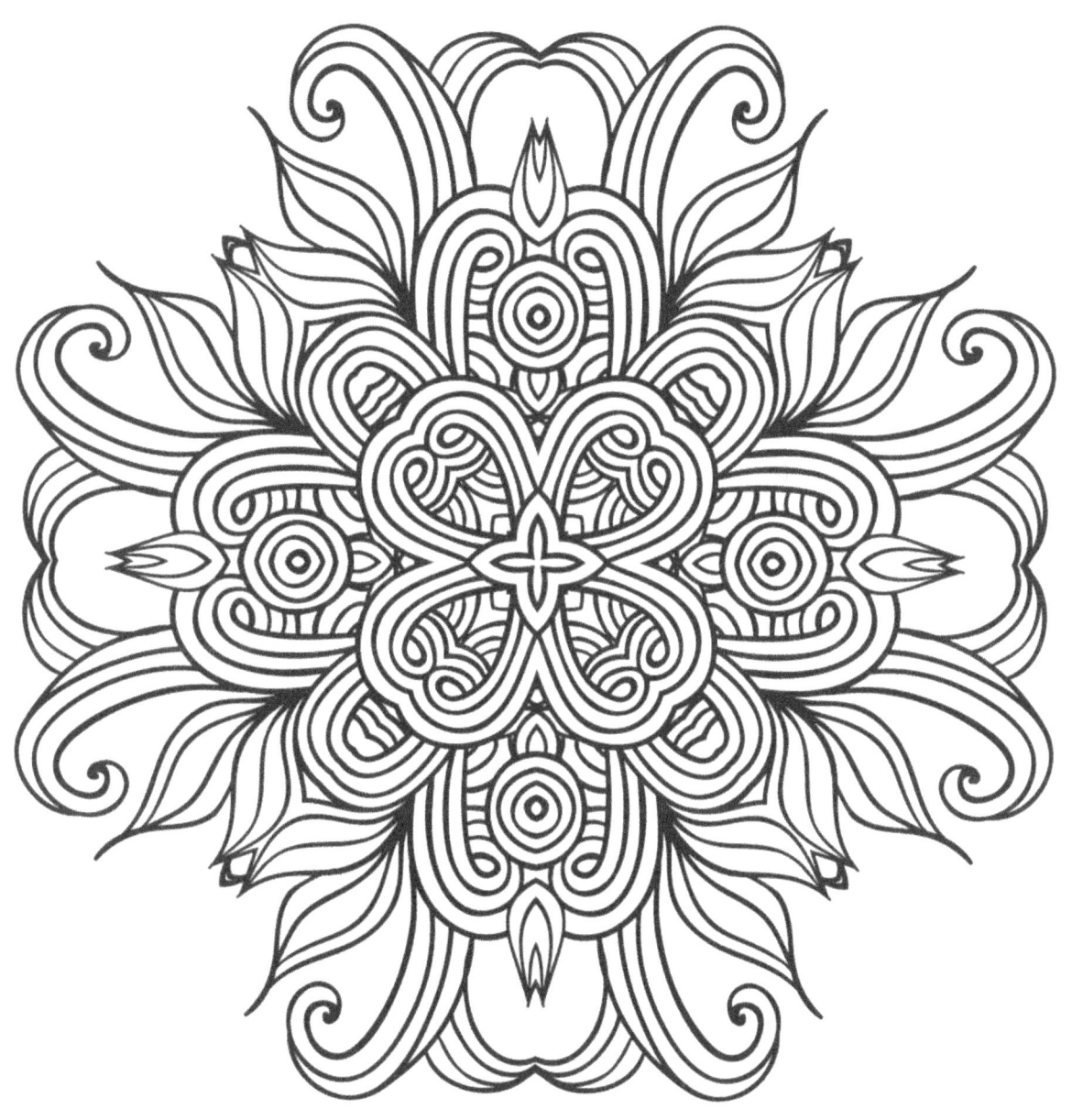

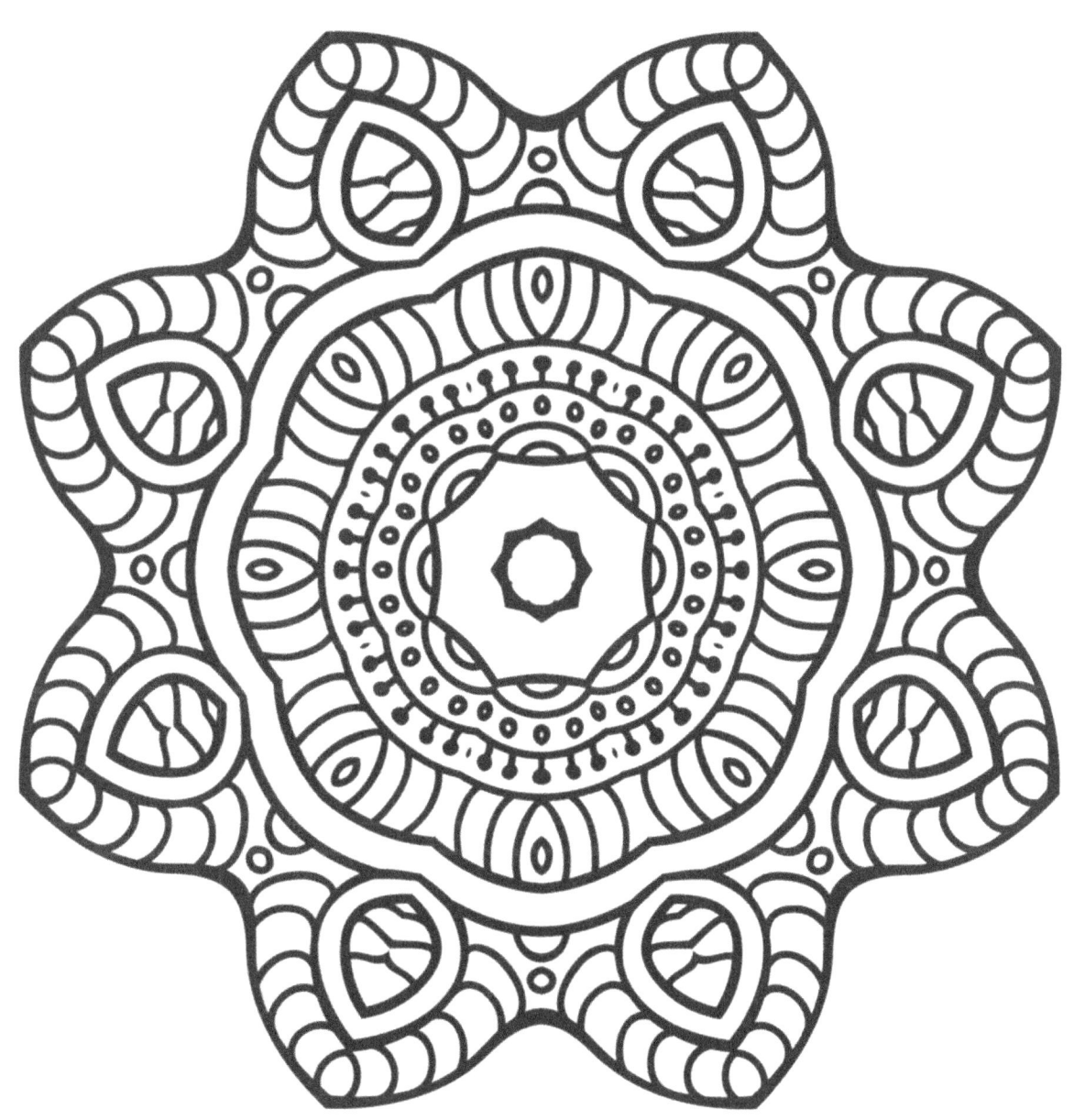

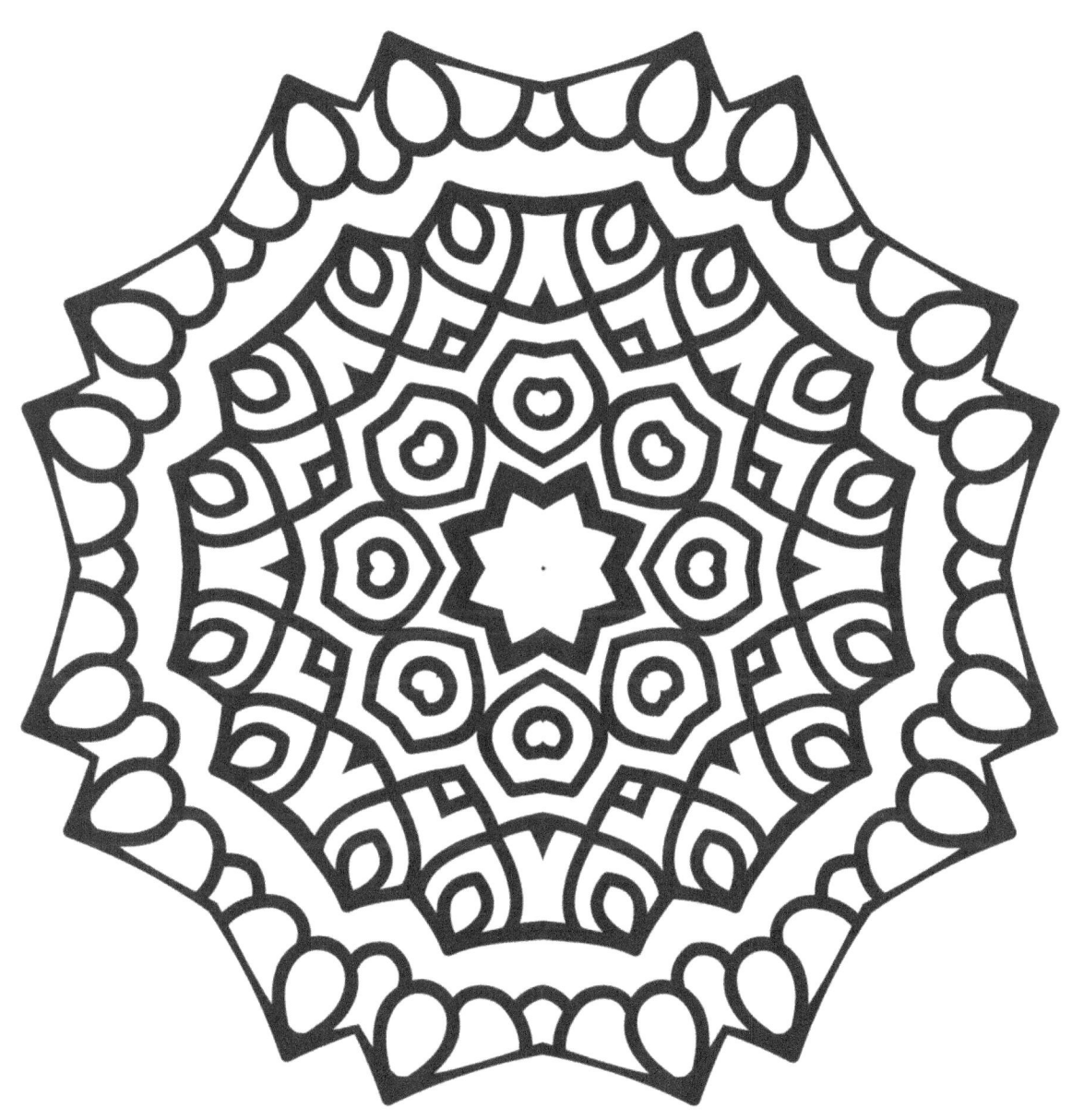

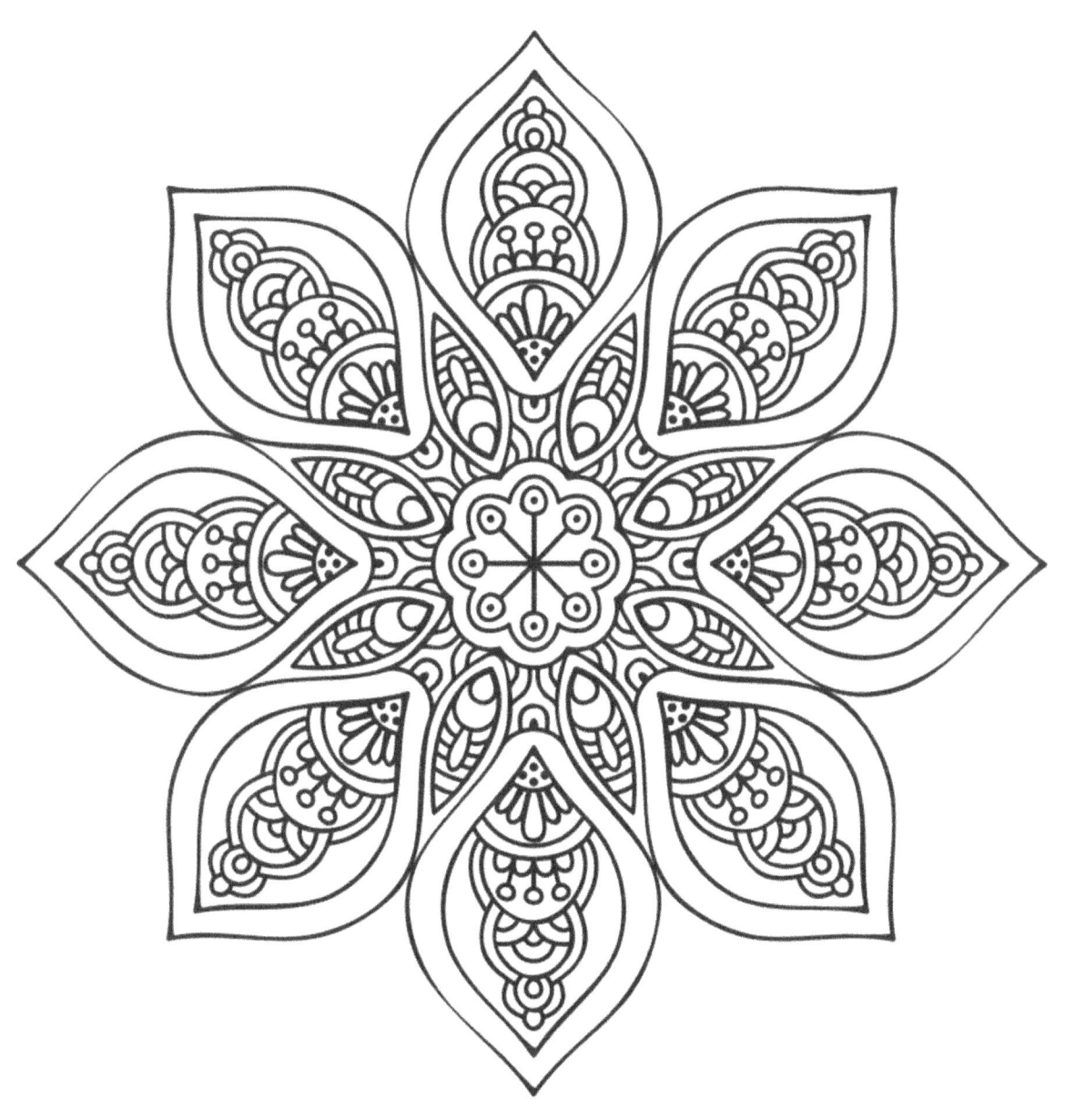

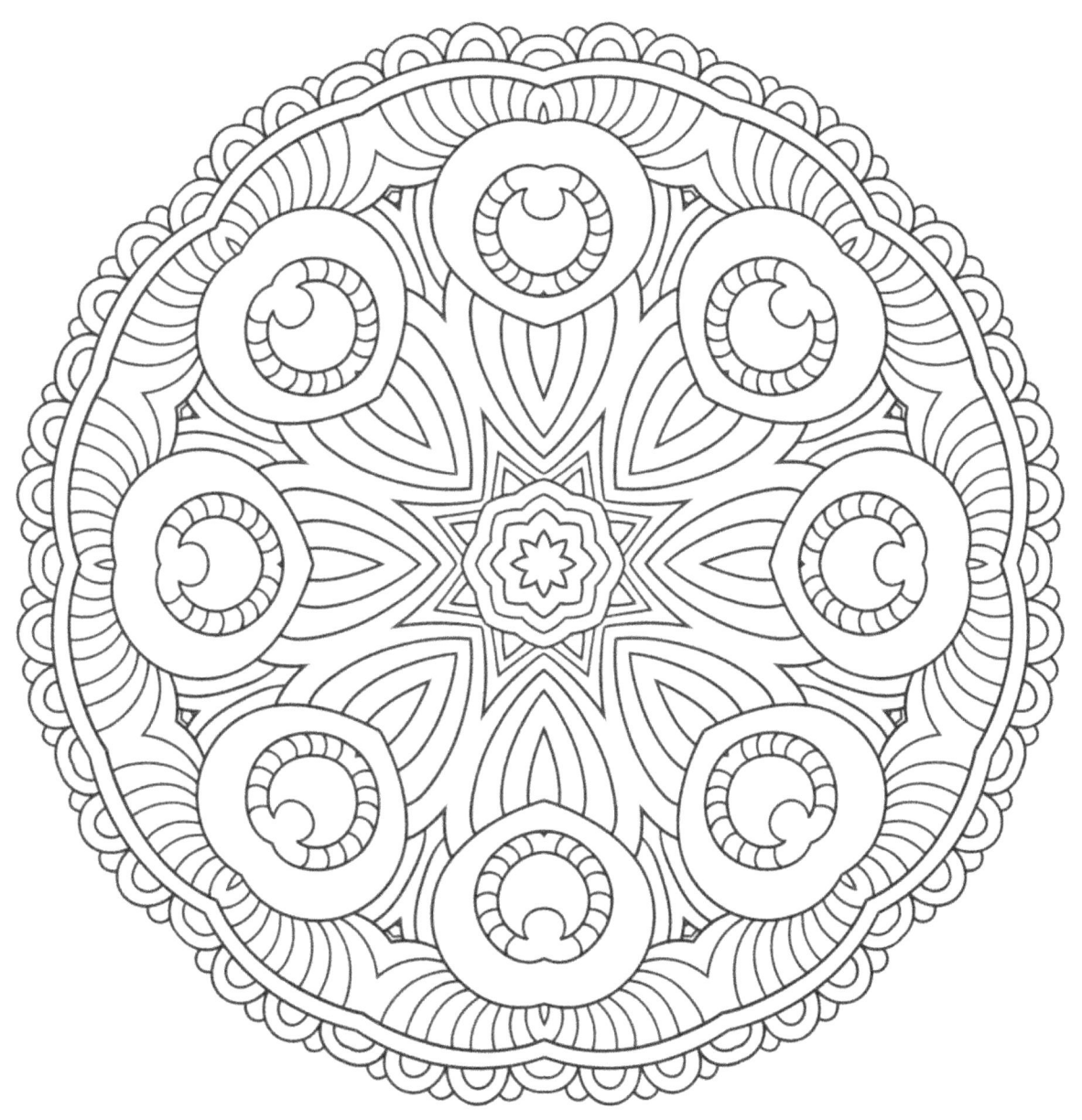

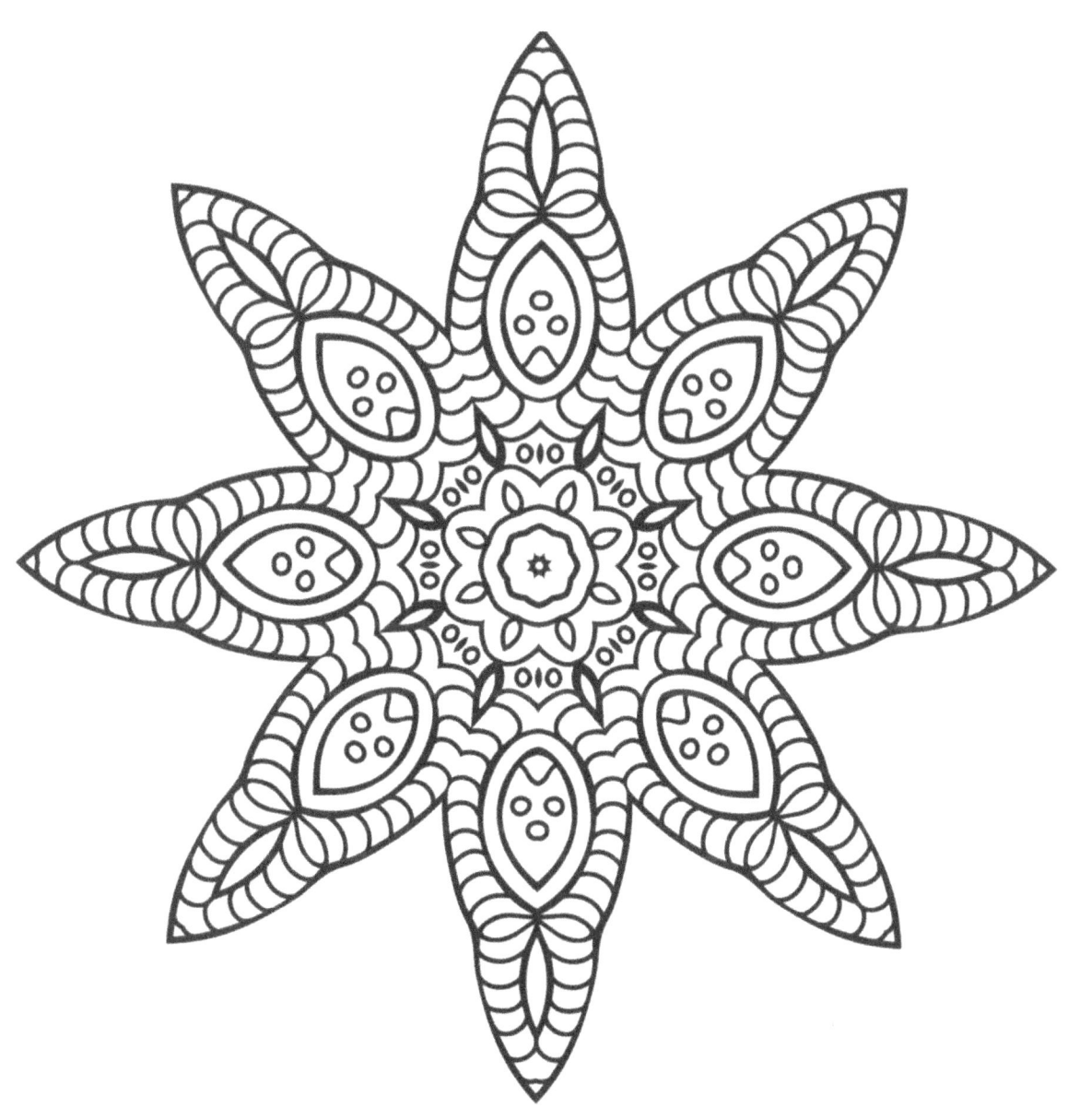

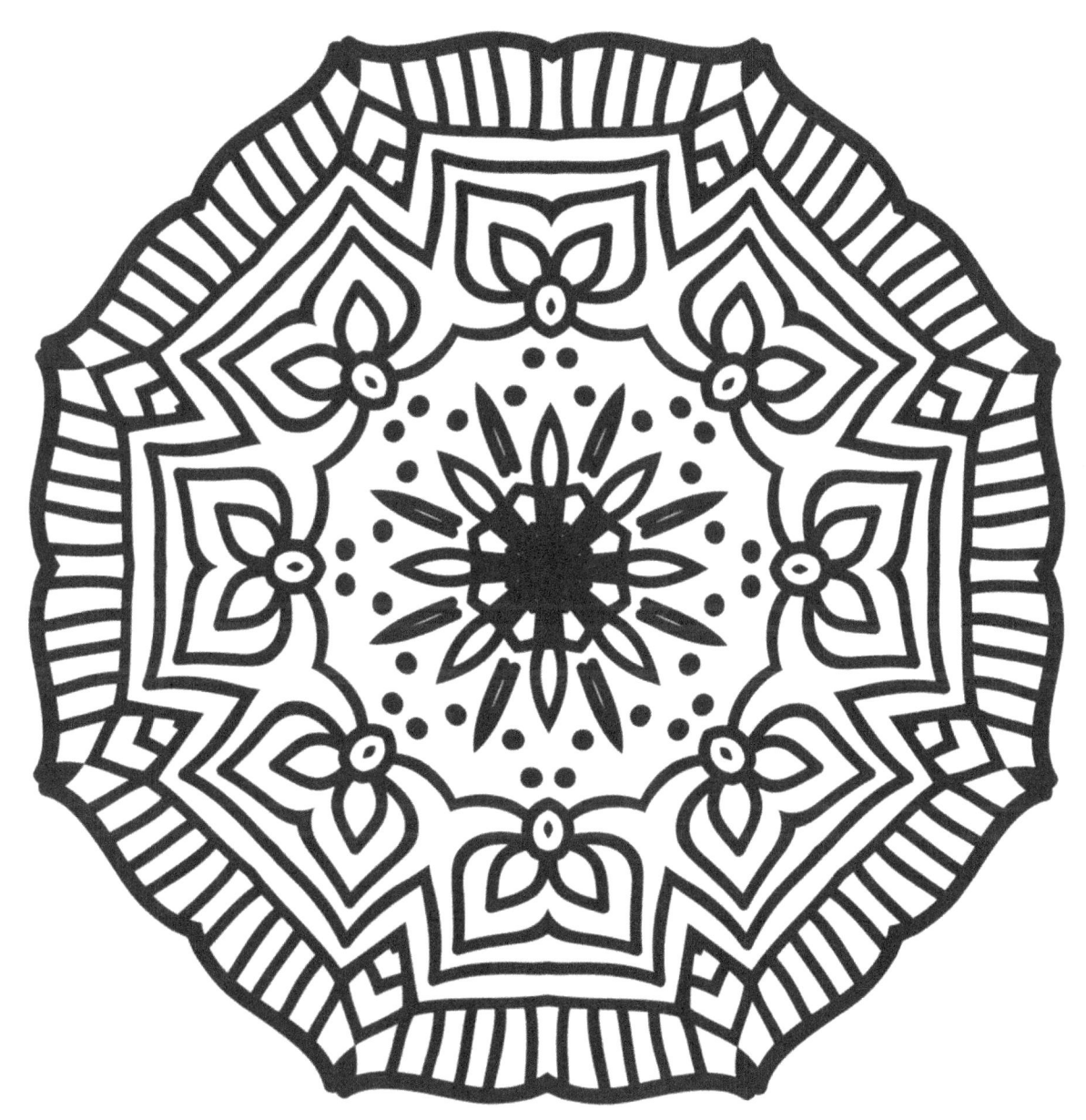

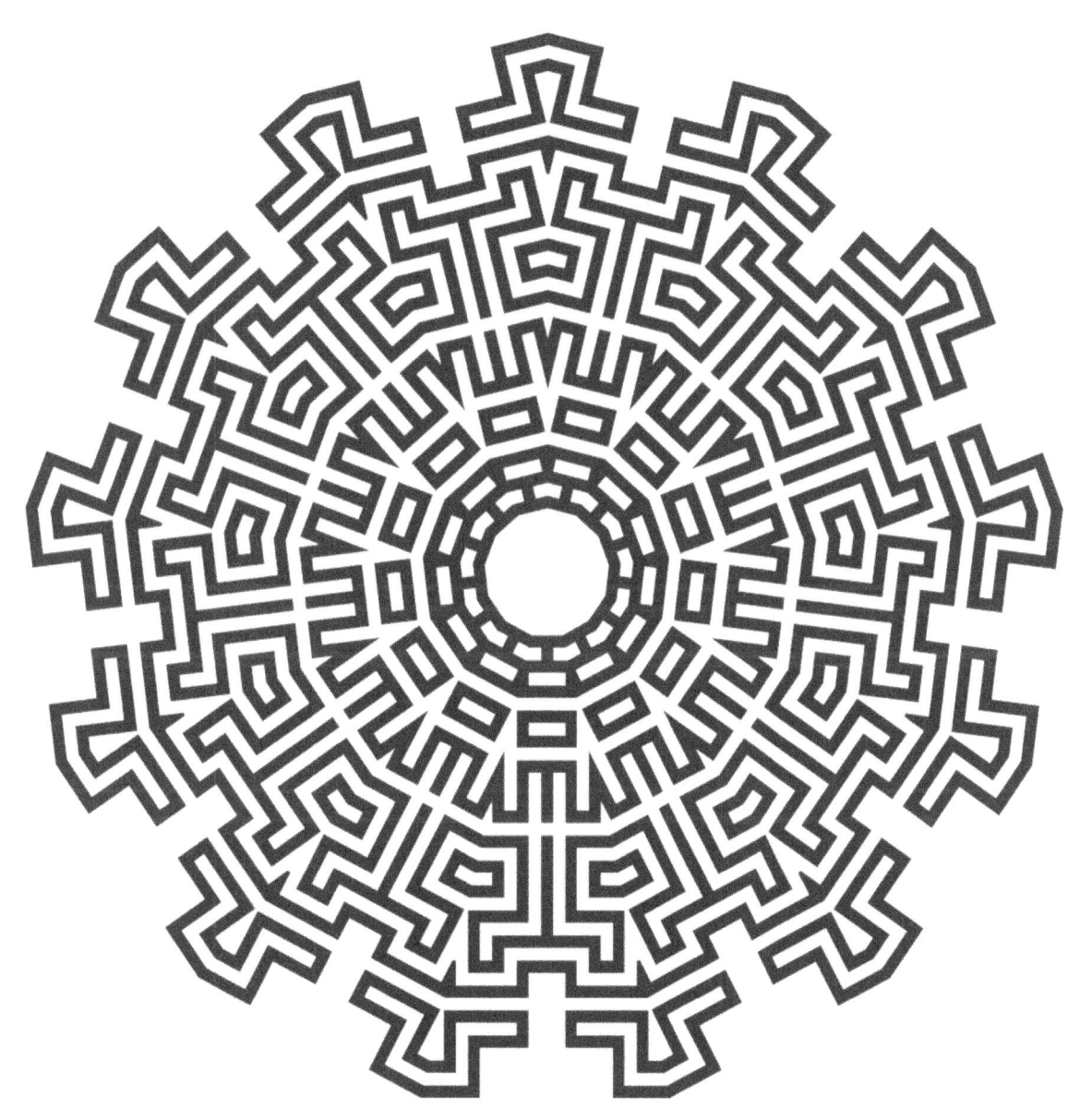

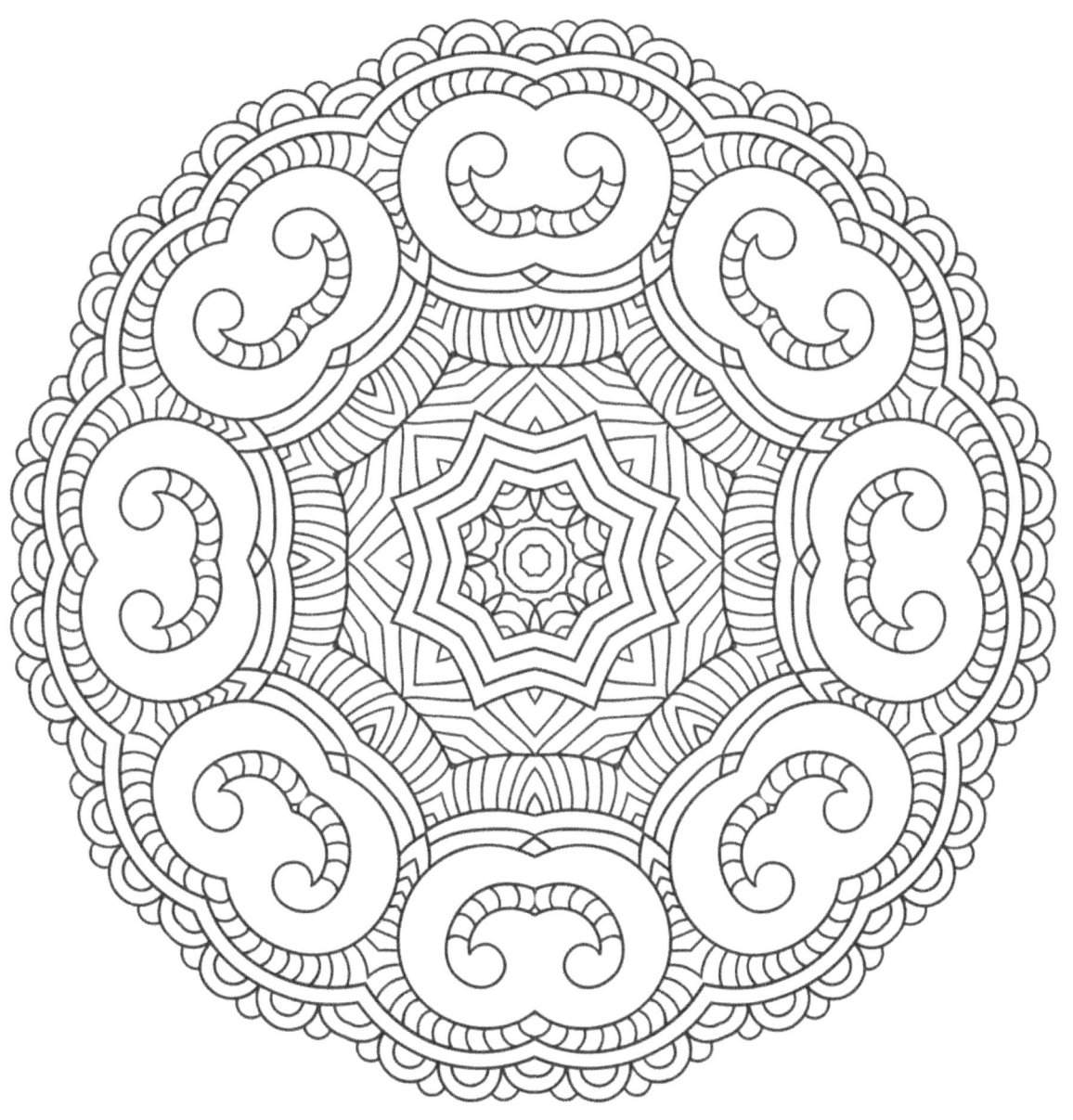

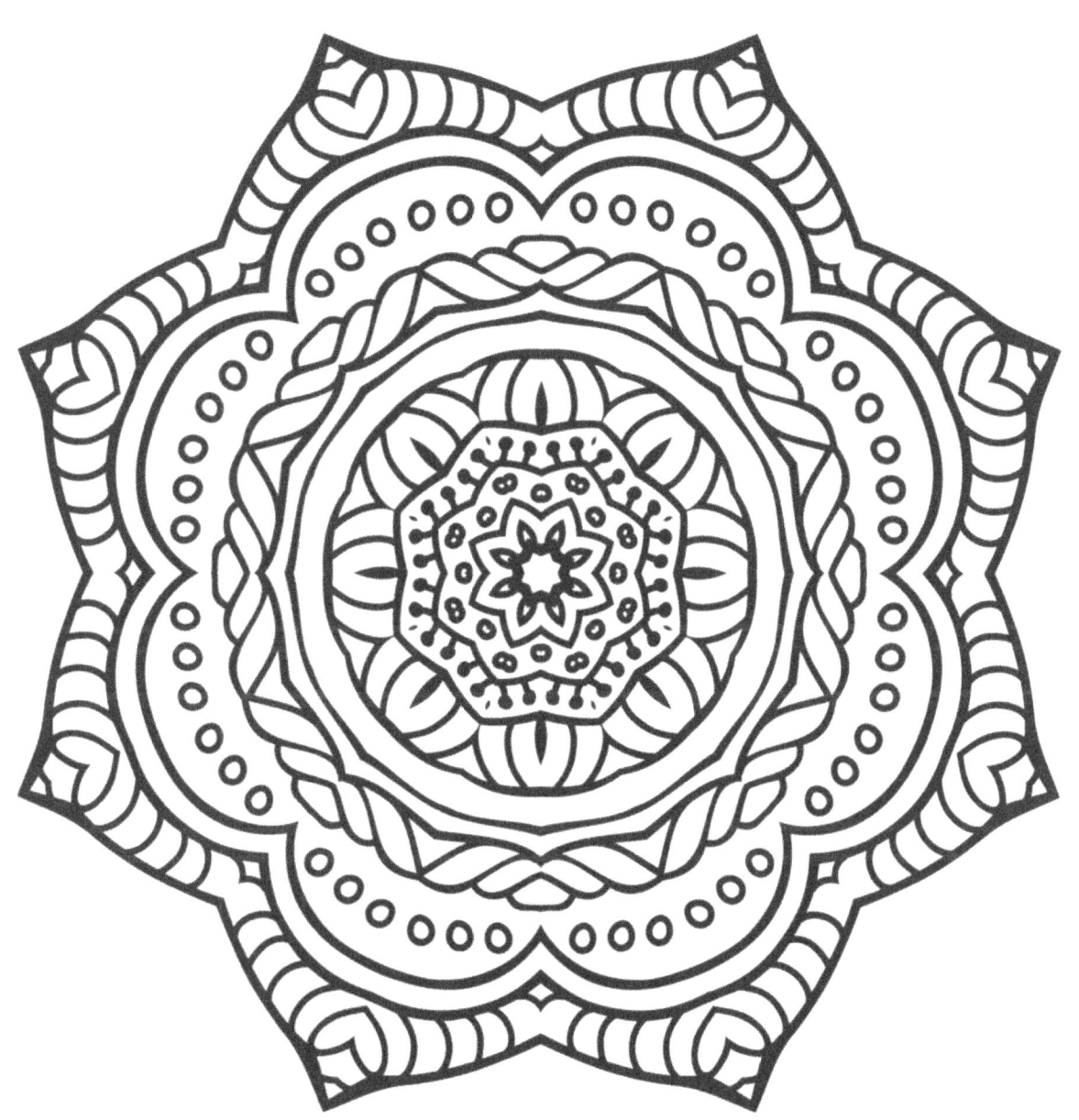

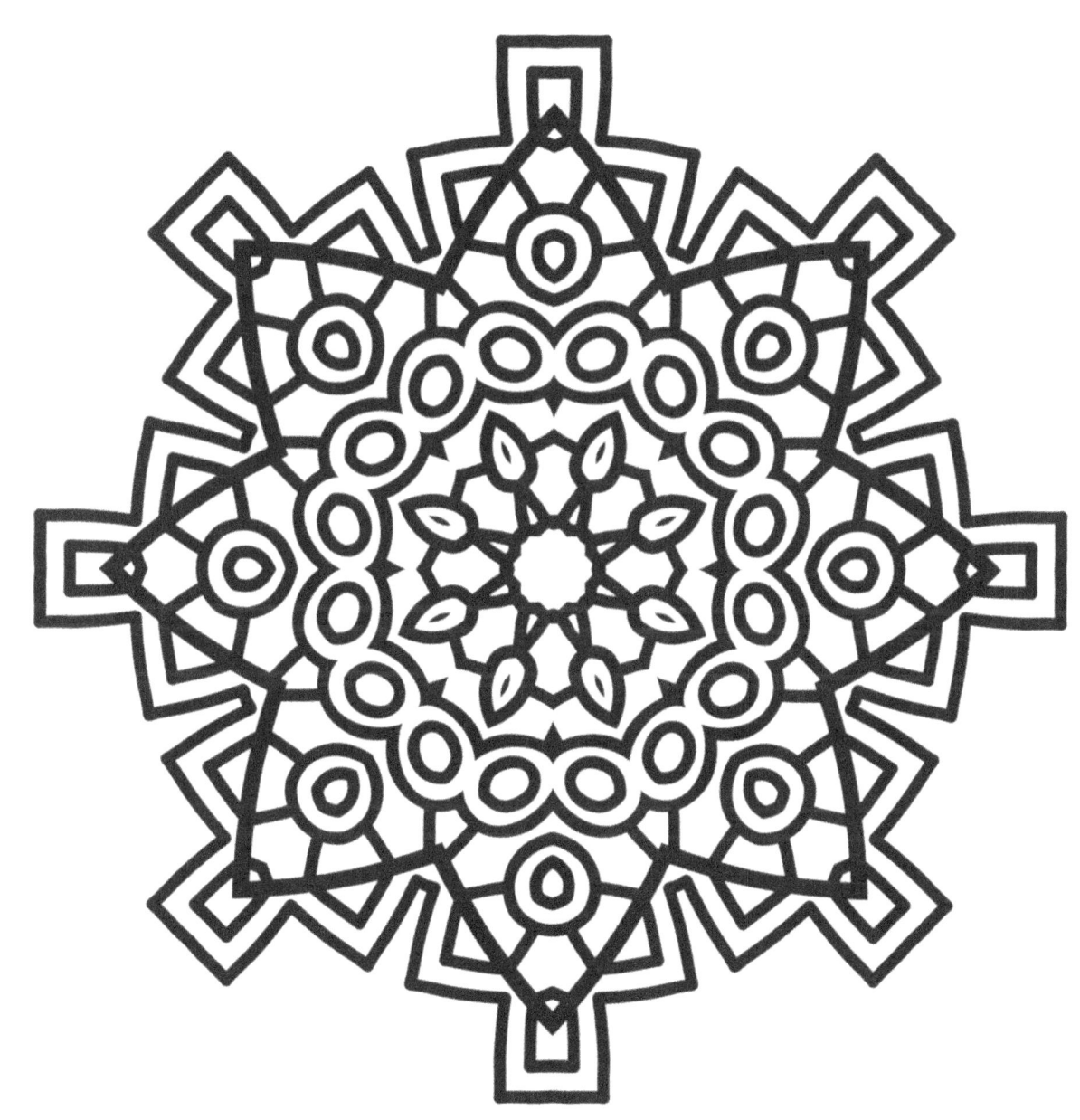

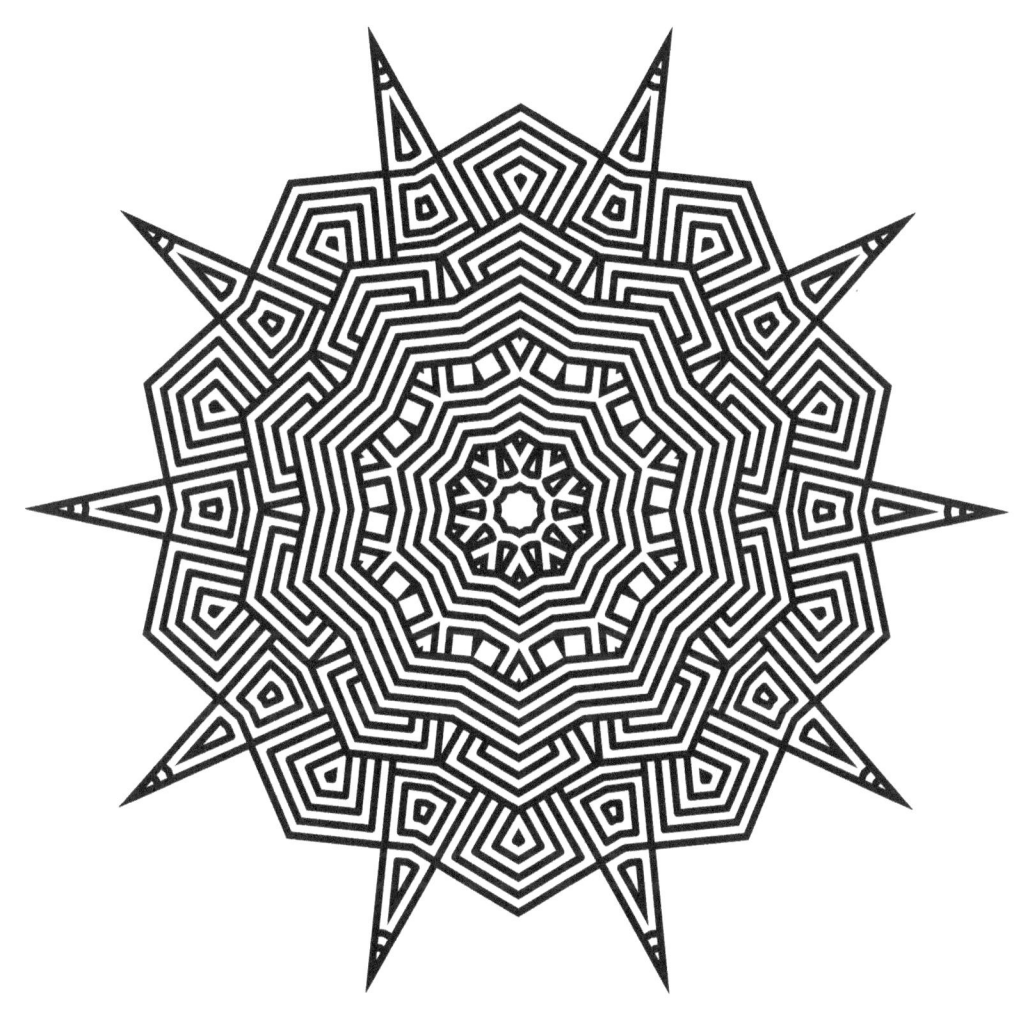

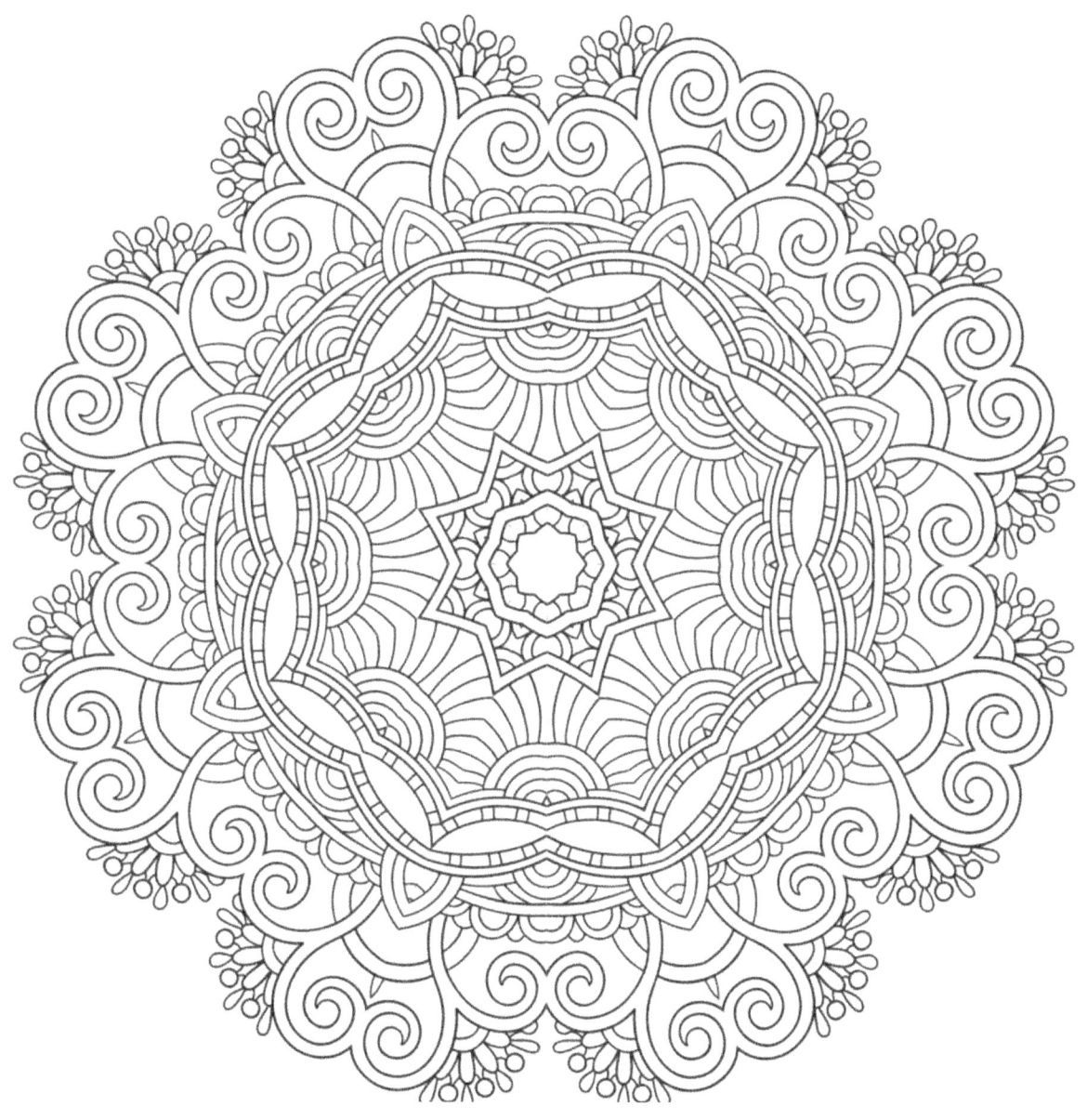

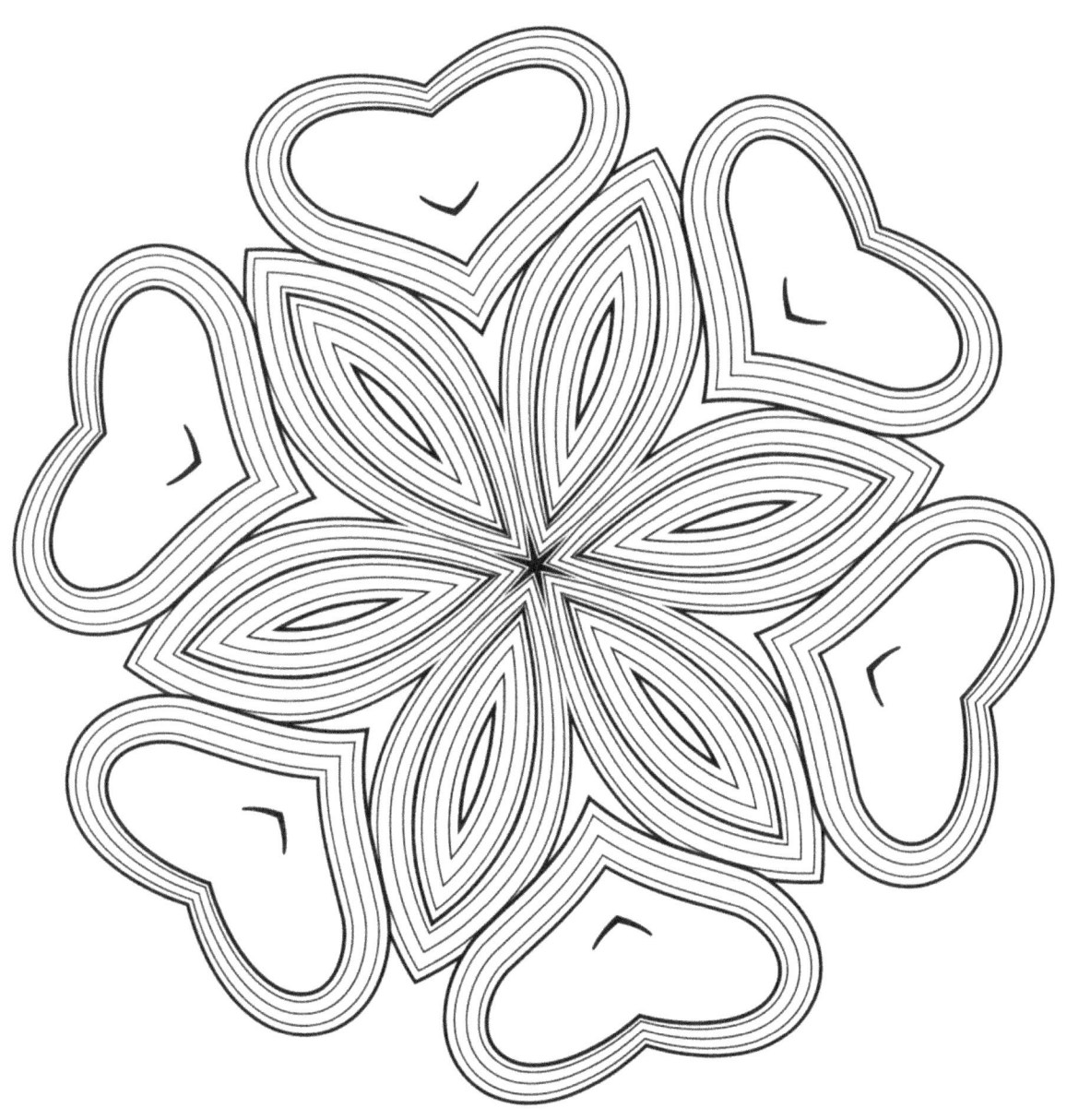

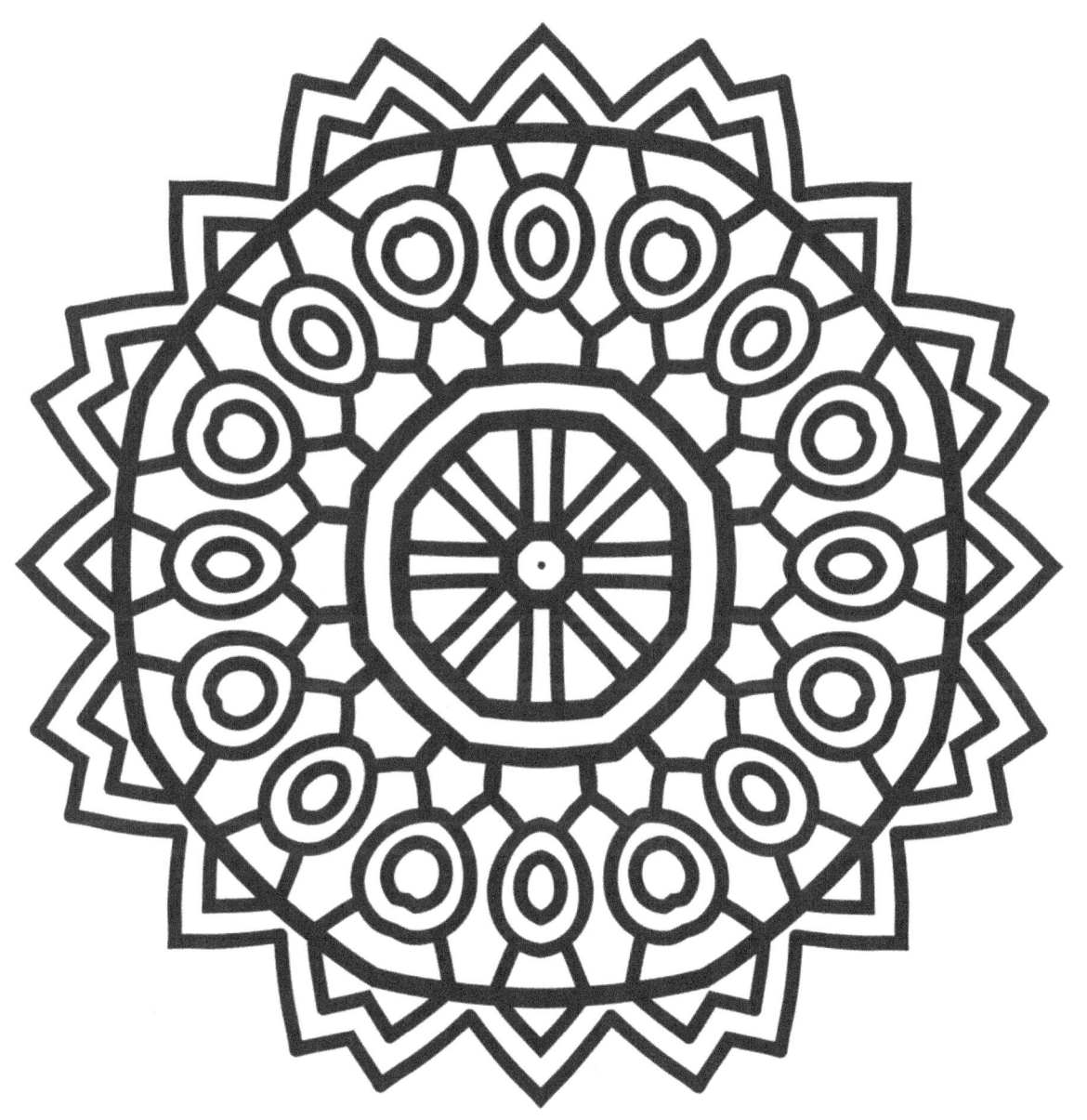

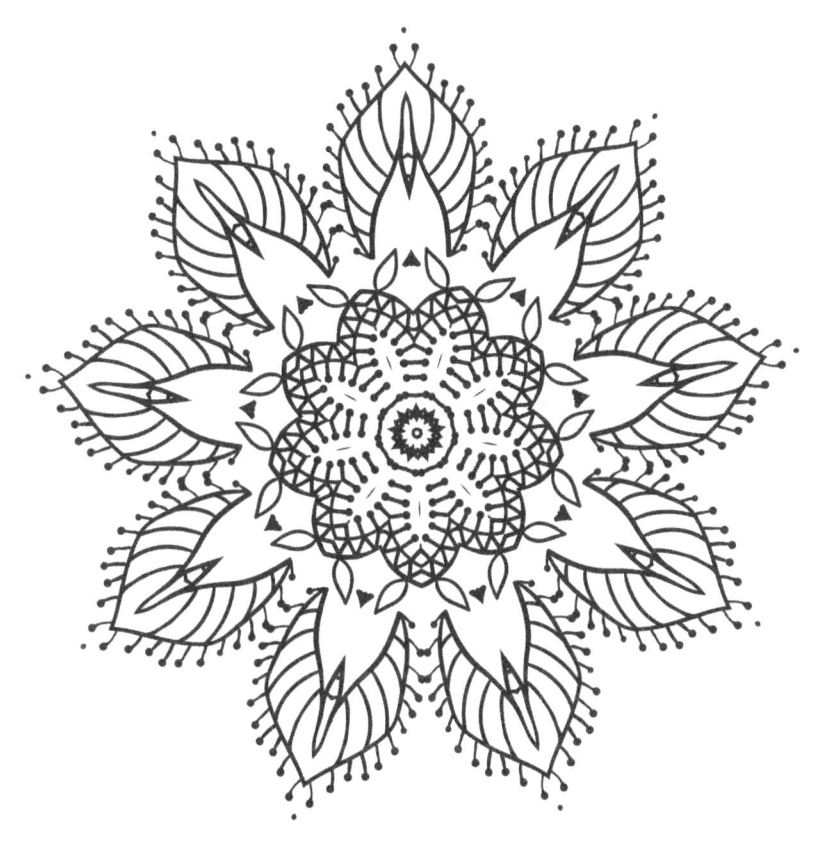

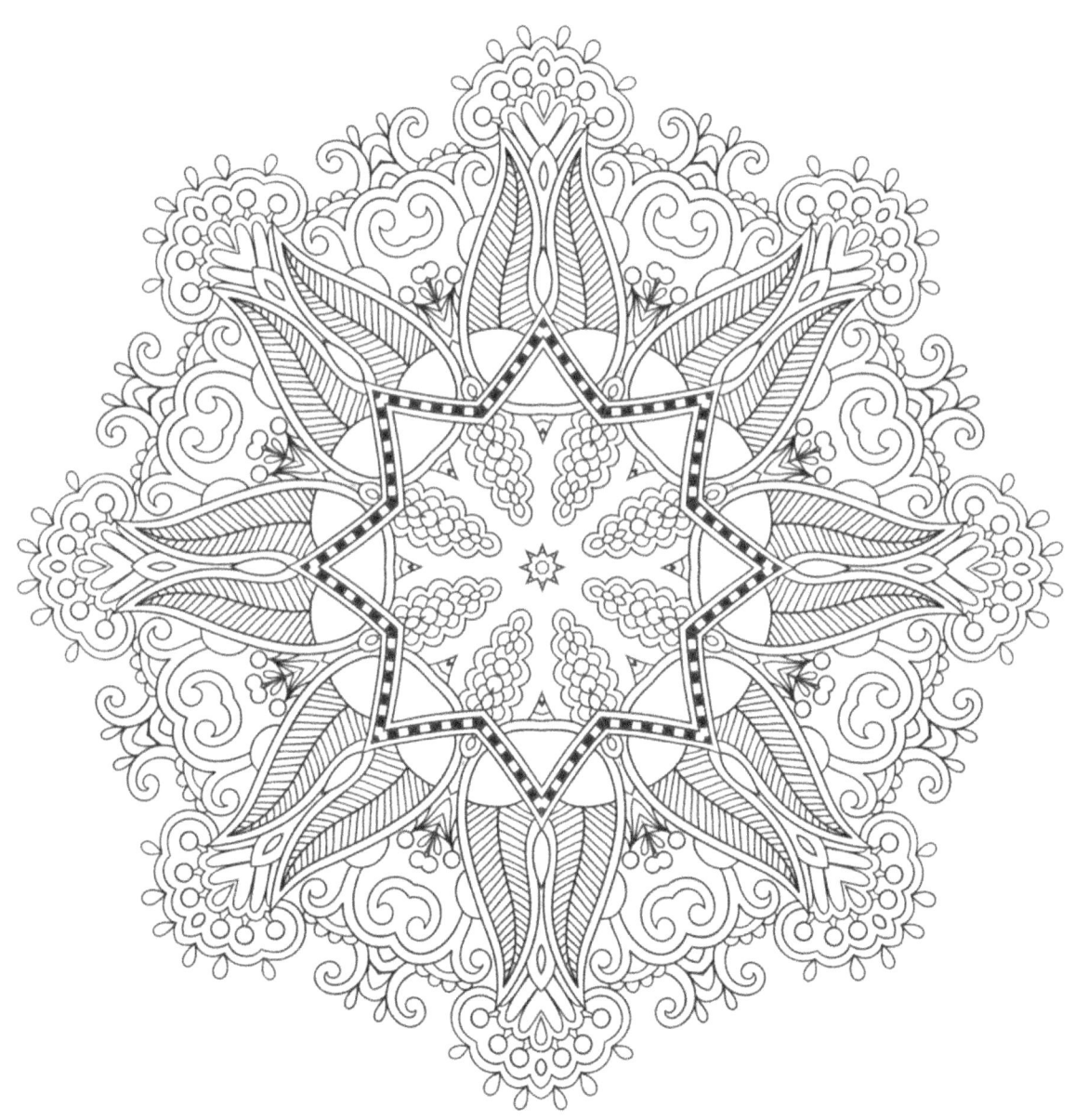

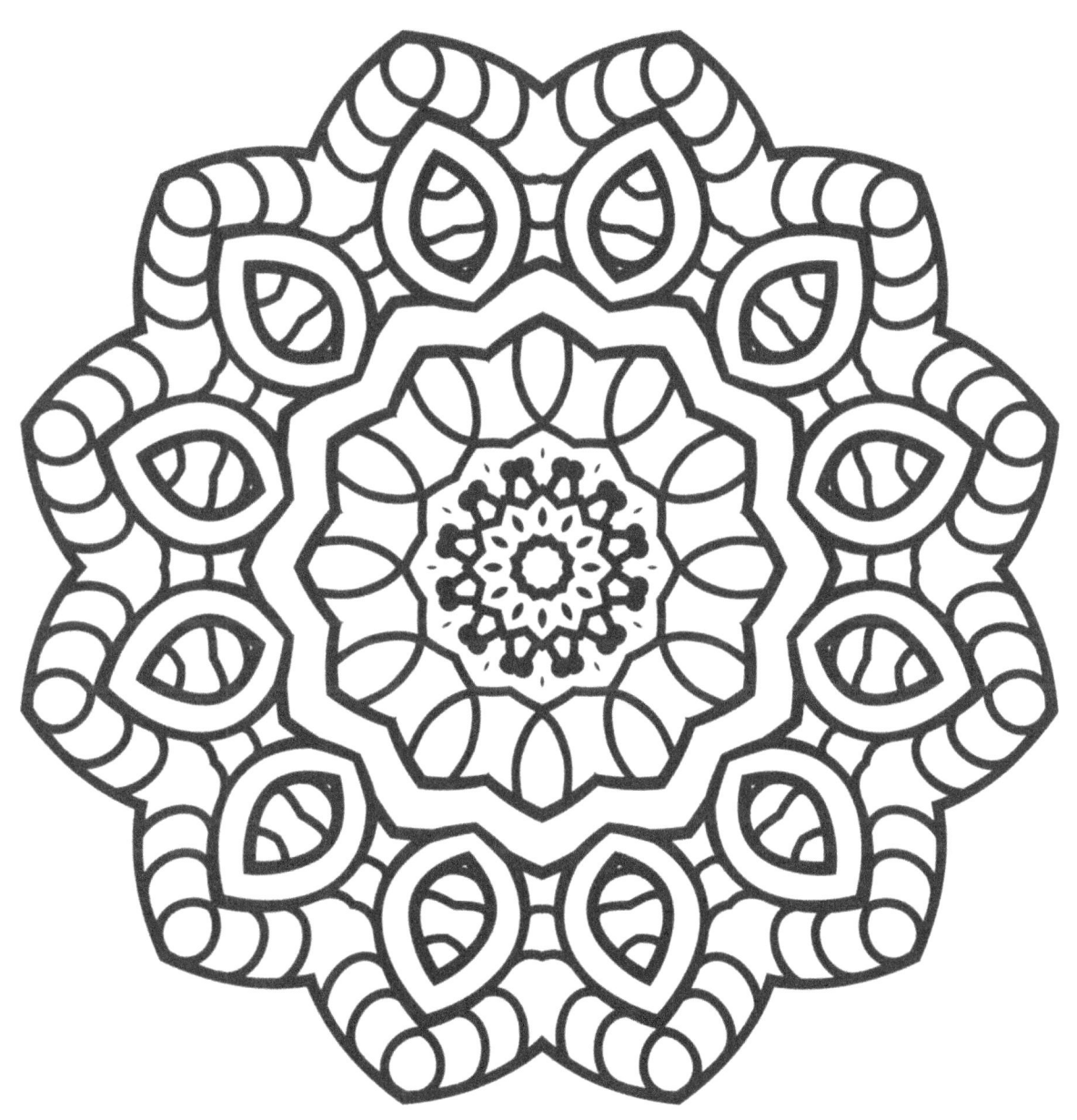

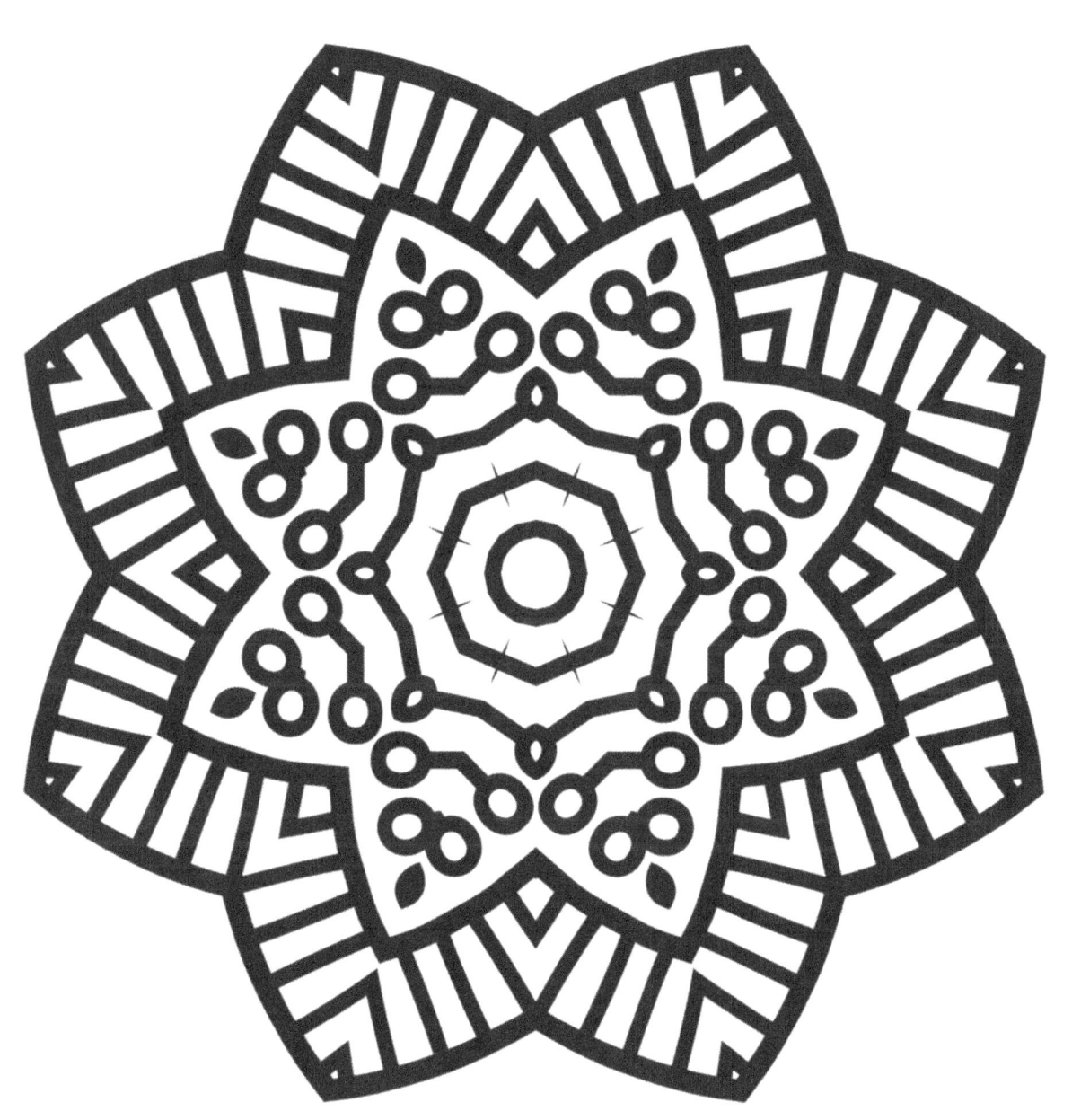

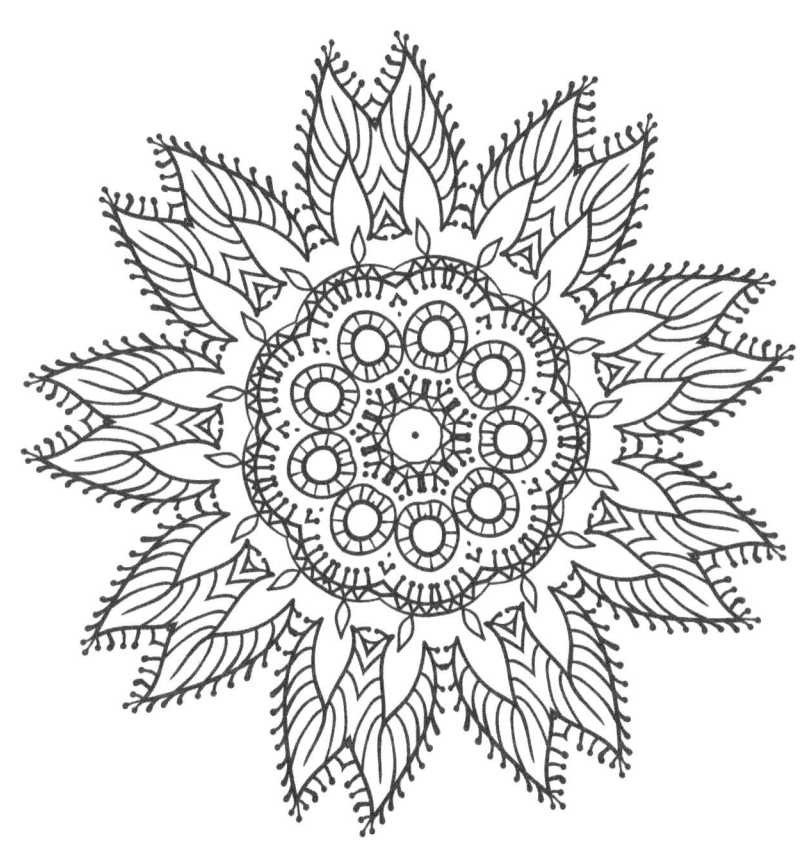

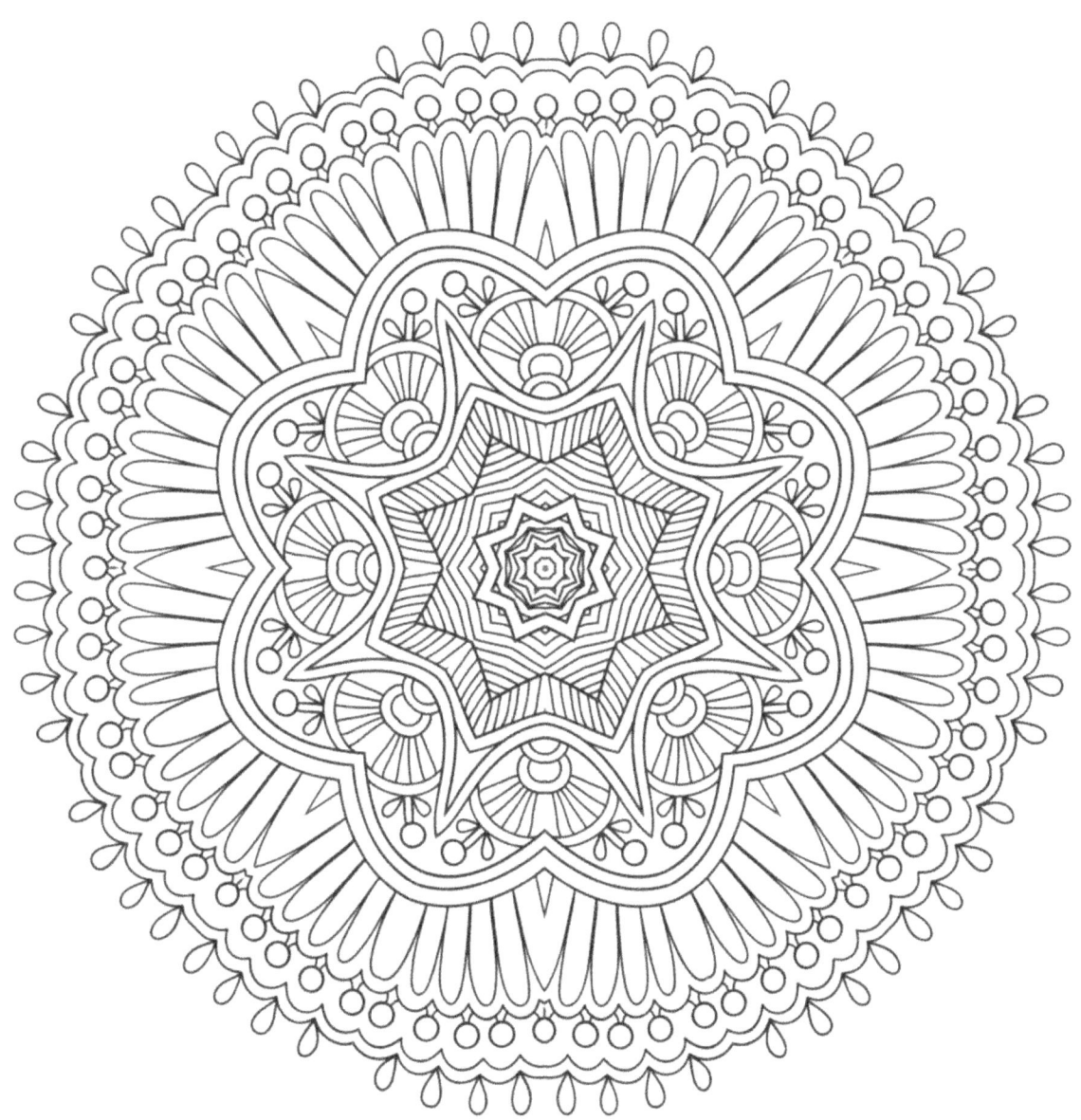

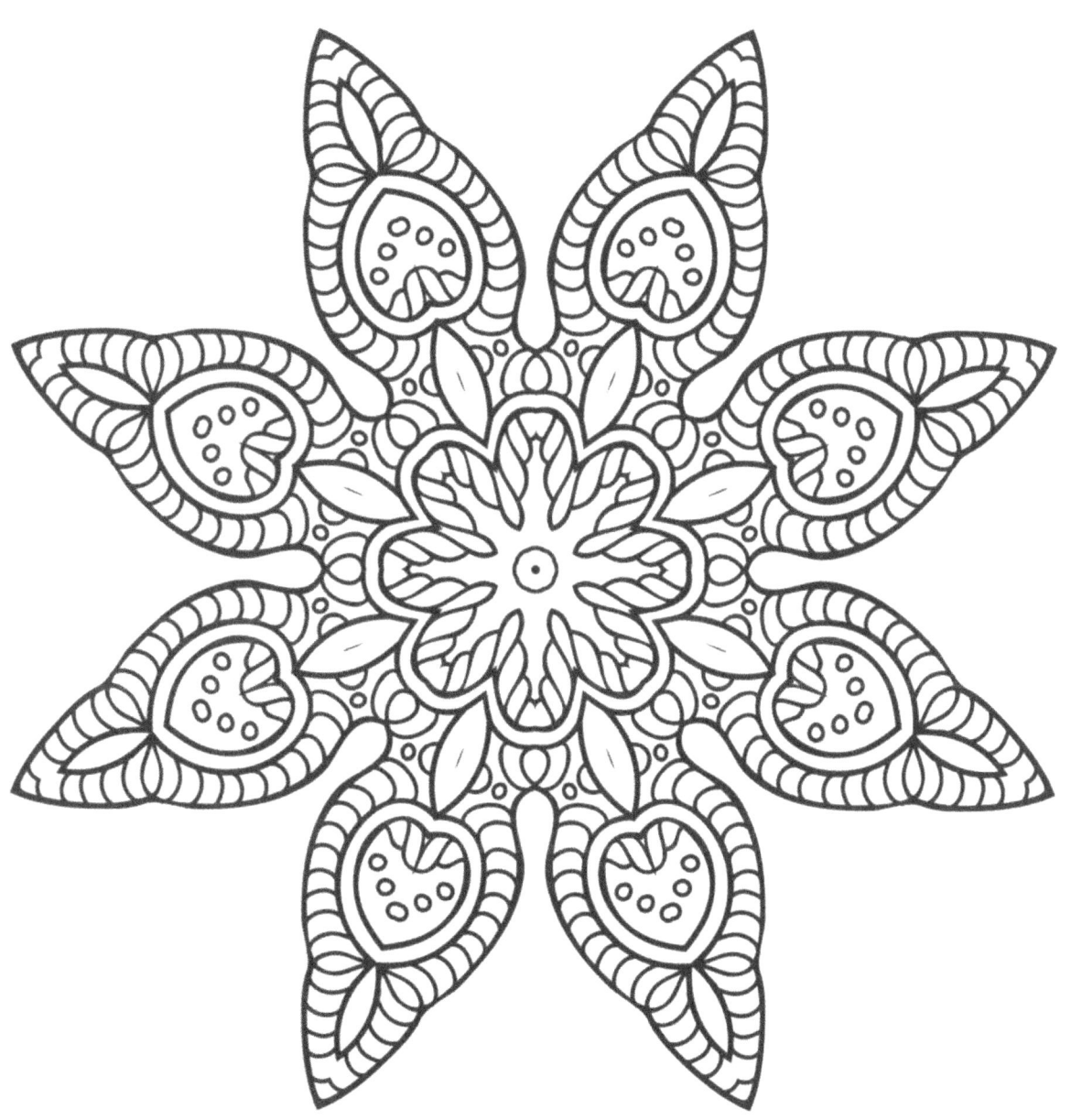

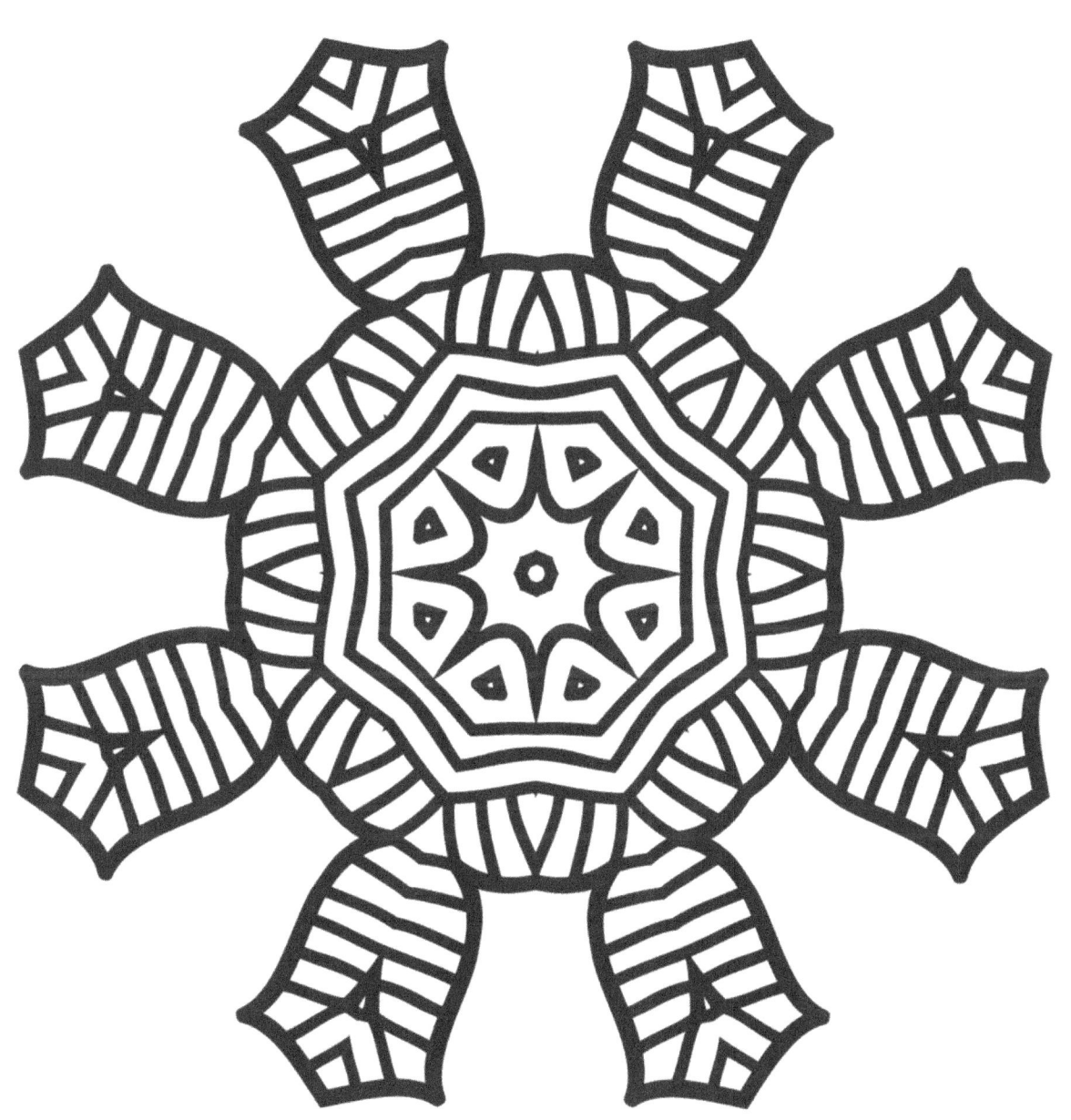

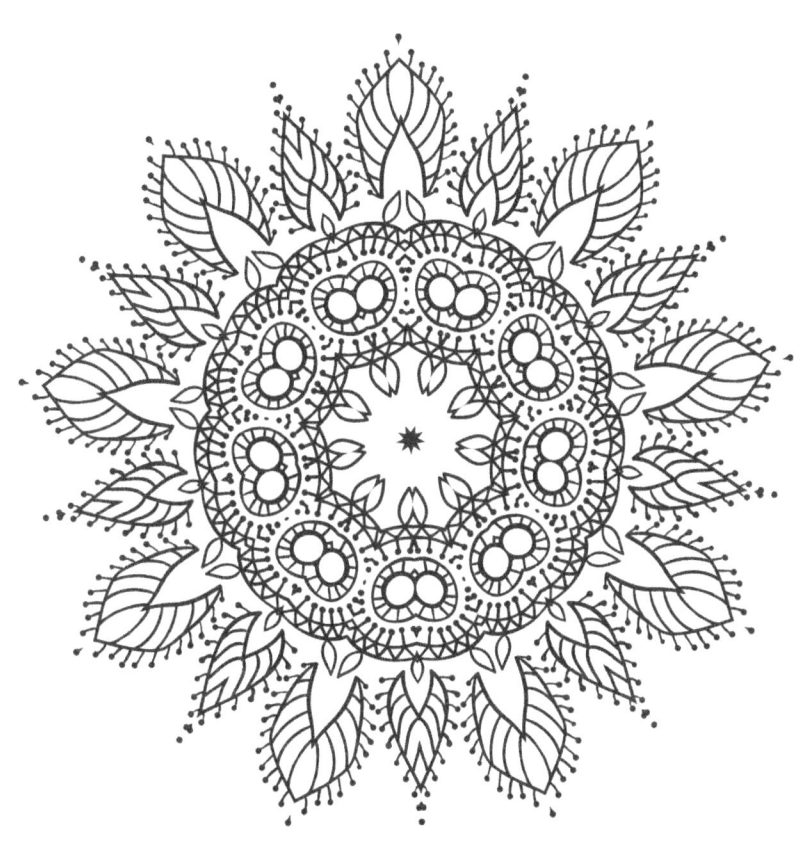

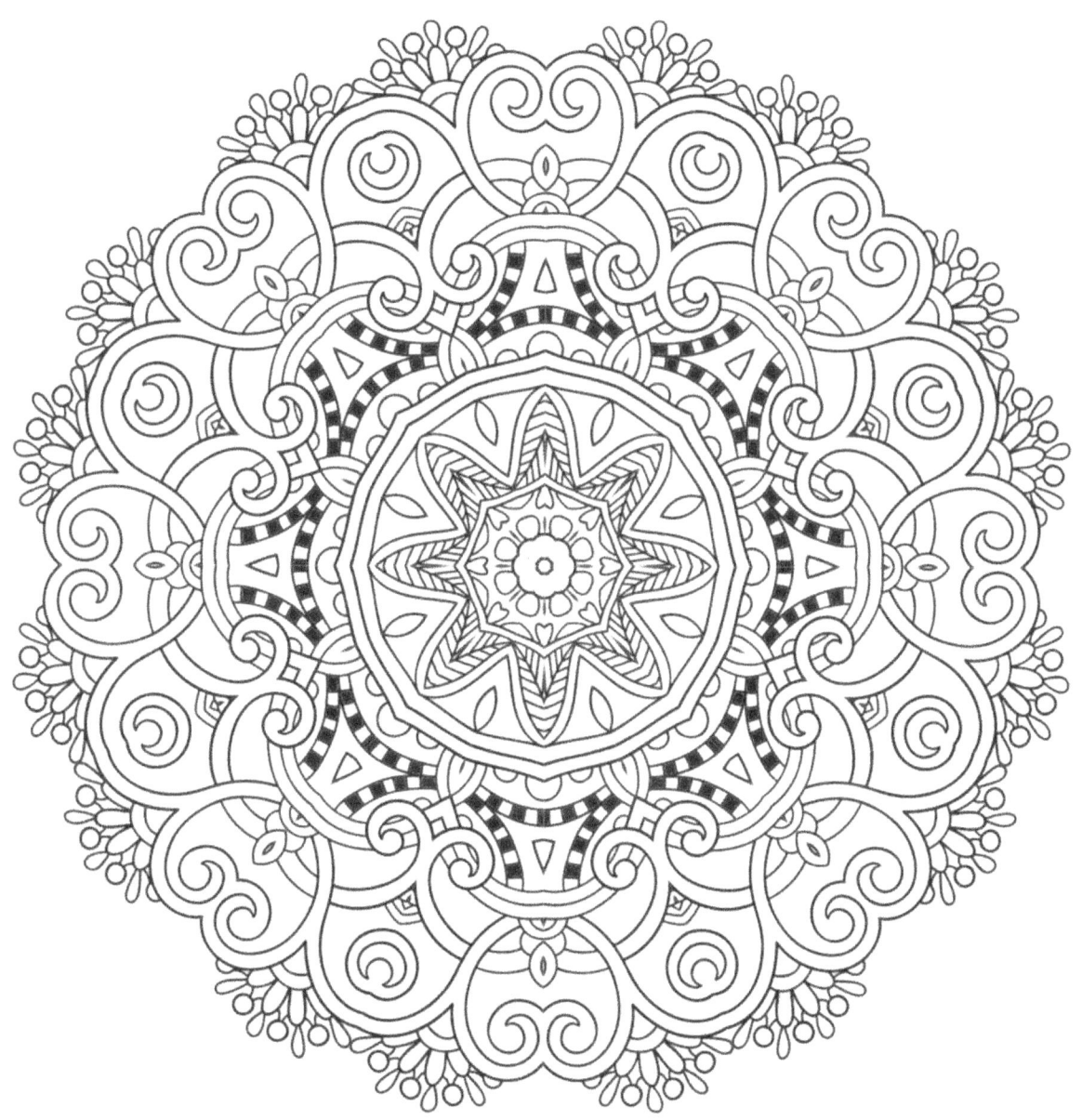

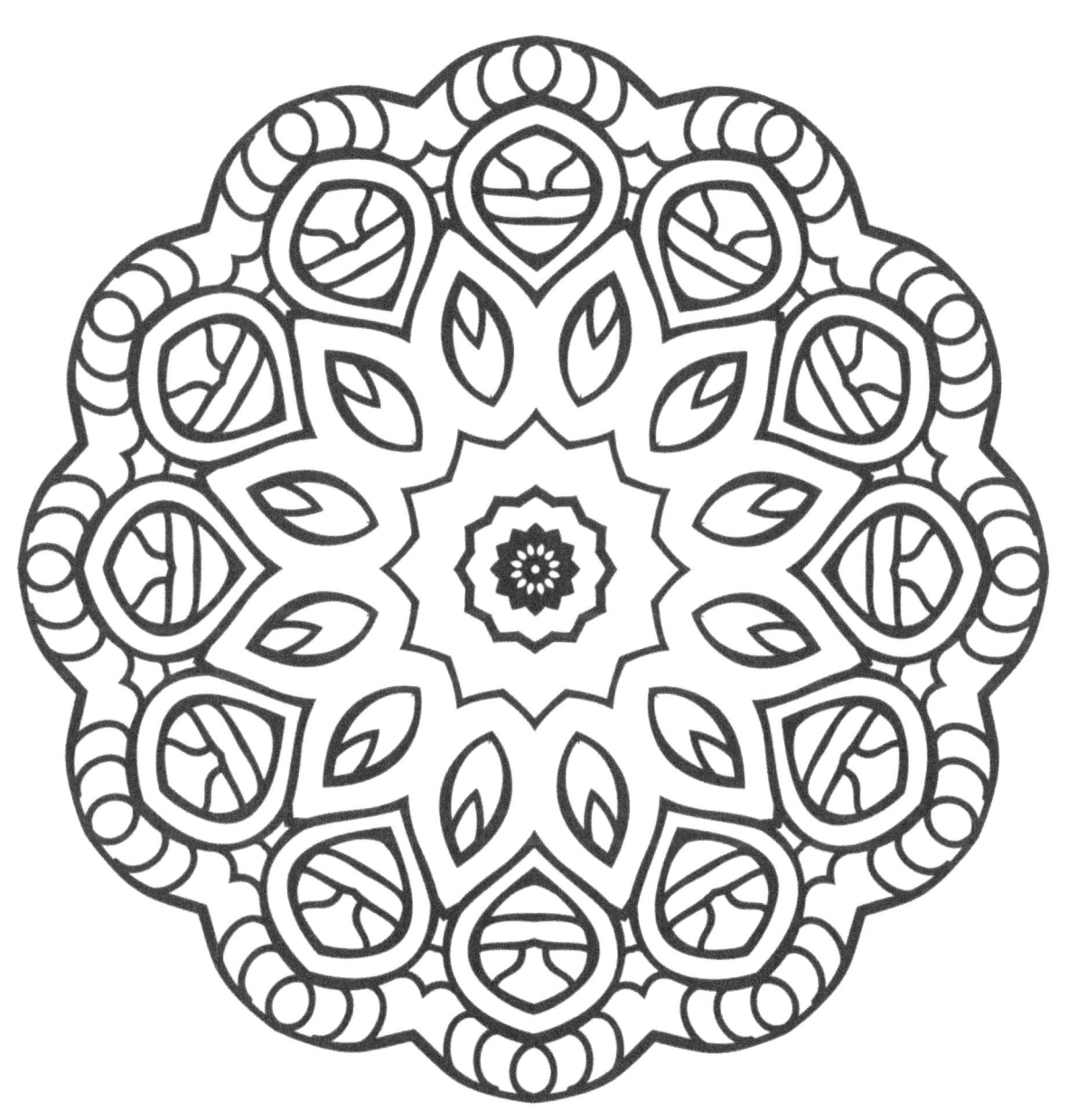

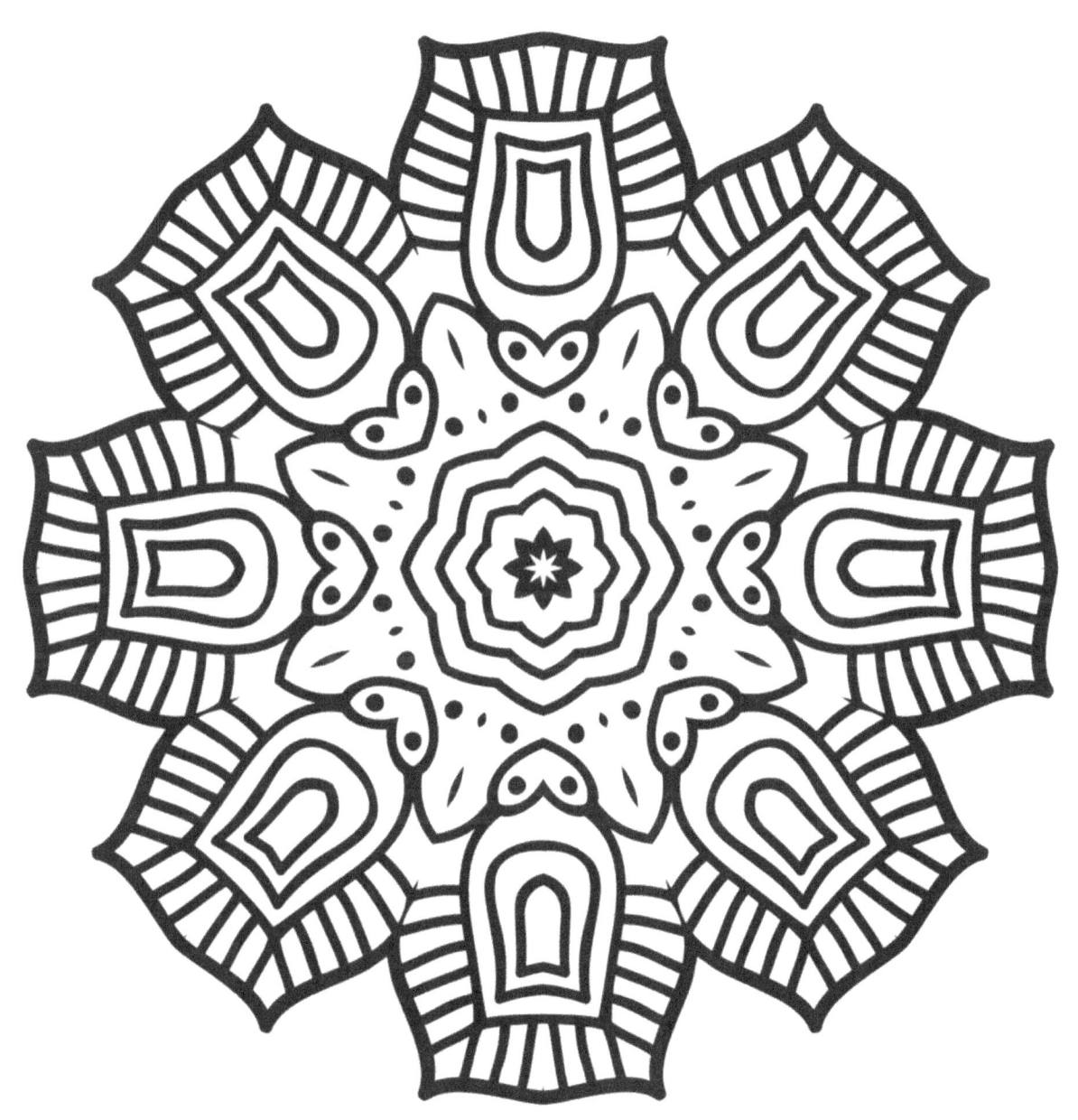

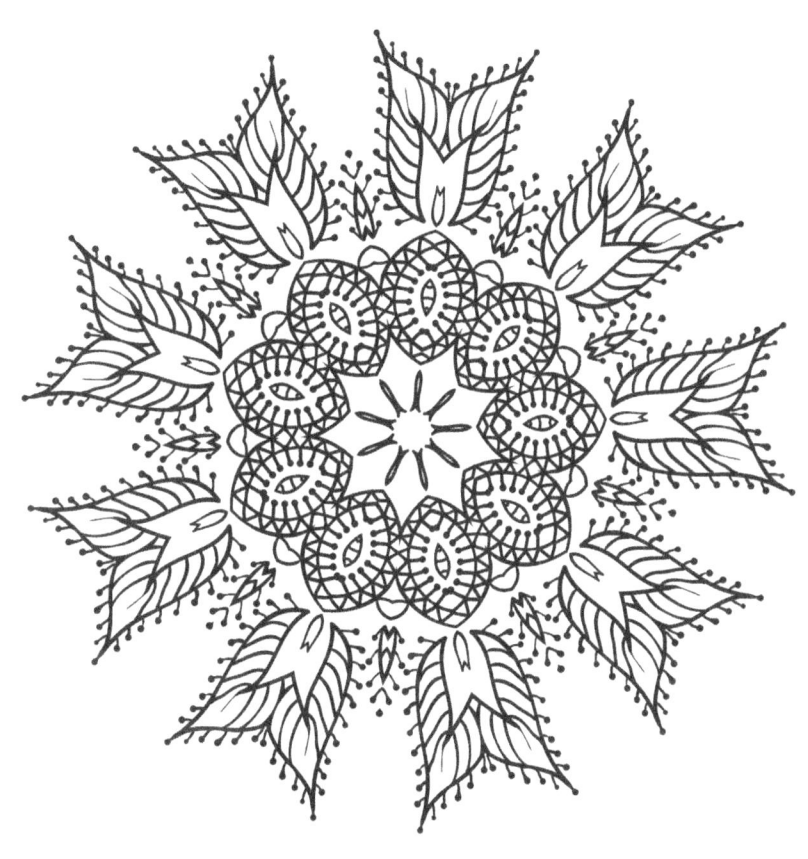

www.ingramcontent.com/pod-product-compliance
Lightning Source LLC
Chambersburg PA
CBHW080827180526
45168CB00006B/2596